To Michael

Thank you for

your support

Blair Bell[illegible]

Doctor Tales

✦

Sketches of the Transformation of American Medicine in the Twentieth Century

Blair Beebe M.D.

iUniverse, Inc.
New York Bloomington

Doctor Tales

Sketches of the Transformation of American Medicine in the Twentieth Century

iUniverse books may be ordered through booksellers or by contacting:

iUniverse
1663 Liberty Drive
Bloomington, IN 47403
www.iuniverse.com
1-800-Authors (1-800-288-4677)

ISBN: 978-0-595-52504-1 (pbk)
ISBN: 978-0-595-51353-6 (cloth)
ISBN: 978-0-595-62557-4 (ebk)

Printed in the United States of America

iUniverse rev. date 10/30/08

For Blair, Helen, John, and Sarah

"The good physician treats the disease; the great physician treats the patient who has the disease."

Sir William Osler (1849–1919)
Physician-in-Chief,
Johns Hopkins Hospital (1889–1910)

Contents

Preface

These stories came from my more than thirty-five years of practice as a physician specializing in internal medicine. Many years have passed since I knew the characters in the tales and experienced the events recounted. Certainly, those years have clouded my memory of the intimate details, but the essentials are there, perhaps without strict authenticity, but with the sympathy, the humor, and the anguish lived.

Most of the people included are no longer living; nevertheless, in order to avoid offending the families of any of my many former acquaintances who may appear in these sketches, I have changed most of the names. I often blended two personalities to create one character, and combined several separate events into one. But the sketches relate events that really happened, and describe doctors, nurses, and patients who really existed. Most of the locations named are where those events actually took place, including Jefferson Medical College, the island of Guam, the Elliot Community Hospital in Keene, New Hampshire, and the Kaiser Permanente Medical Center in San Jose, California.

The last tale, "Influenza," is a short story that takes place in Davis, California, and is about a fictional epidemic based on real avian flu outbreaks that occurred in Southeast Asia between 2004 and 2006. The guidelines for "social distancing" mentioned in the story were actually published by the Center for Disease Control in 2007, as was the document labeled "National Strategy for Pandemic Influenza" signed by the president.

My career was varied, perhaps more so than for most physicians, hence the reason for the variety of situations in *Doctor Tales*. I was a flight surgeon in the navy during the war in Vietnam, practiced for a time in New England, held clinical faculty appointments at Dartmouth and Stanford, was chief of staff of a large hospital in California, and served as associate executive director of the Permanente Medical Group in the Northern California region. These are the stories that I remember best.

Blair Beebe, MD
Portola Valley, California
2008

Acknowledgment

Dr. William Spangler, DVM, veterinary pathologist and former professor of veterinary medicine at the University of California, Davis, provided valuable technical advice in writing "Influenza."

Introduction

Doctor Tales consists of fourteen sketches about people and events associated with doctors and hospitals beginning with some of my first impressions and experiences as a twenty-one-year-old medical student at Jefferson Medical College in Philadelphia. I entered medical school in 1959 just before one of the most explosive decades of advances in medical and surgical treatment. Those developments drove the overarching theme of most of the tales: the transition of medicine from a family doctor emphasis in small communities in the first half of the twentieth century, to a more urban, specialized, technology-centered discipline during the second half. Small "cottage hospitals," like Elliot Community Hospital in one of the sketches, still existed in small towns everywhere in 1959, but big, modern, technology-laden medical centers were going to replace them during the 1960s and early 1970s.

Industrial and technological progress affected medical care in a way that paralleled cultural changes in American life, including the great migration from rural areas to urban centers beginning in the late nineteenth century and peaking just after World War II. Americans no longer lived in the same community where they were born; families spread out across the country in search of jobs or a different lifestyle. Neighborhoods, which had been so important in the early twentieth century, became almost irrelevant, and many people didn't even know their neighbors. Computer screens and handheld devices physically isolated us from one another; the characters on our television screens supplied an electronic family that replaced our biological families in our new spectator-oriented society. We craved perpetual entertainment. Associations that were tentative and quickly terminated replaced long-term relationships between people. One major casualty of this new culture was the decline in long-term doctor-patient relationships and trust.

My intention was to present important themes in medicine during this transition, beginning with some divergent medical education philosophies about how best to train physicians. Up to the middle of the twentieth century, doctors thought of medical practice as more of an art, but with the huge emphasis on research and technological advances after World War II, medicine transformed itself into a science. In doing so, treatment outcomes improved, including some in spectacular fashion, but only at the cost of a more specialized—and more impersonal—system. Doctors before World War II were preoccupied with disease prevention and health promotion, but later we disdained prevention in favor of impressive new treatments and procedures, such as antibiotics, cardiac pacemakers, open-heart surgery, transplants, lasers, and many others.

The advent of Medicare in the 1960s brought with it a payment system that amounted to a blank check from the government made out to doctors and hospitals for diagnostic and treatment procedures, but providing not one cent for prevention. The economic incentives and prestige of being on the leading edge pushed young physicians into new, exciting, procedure-oriented specialties and away from the more mundane life of a general practitioner. Hospitals swelled with patients, and physicians—who had previously lived in communities and neighborhoods next to their patients—moved their offices adjacent to hospitals to take on the aura of the specialist. Patients with backaches or sprained knees shunned general practitioners in favor of "the best" orthopedic surgeon, and for some patients, only an ENT surgeon would do for the most basic seasonal allergy problem.

Two important consequences of this transformation developed into major social issues for the twenty-first century: an epidemic of self-destructive health habits and a healthcare system with runaway costs. Advertising and Hollywood films promoted the glamour of tobacco use, which spread to more than one-third of adults causing lung cancer, emphysema, and a boost in the incidence in heart attacks.

A higher standard of living, more efficient agricultural production, and the promotion of convenient, high-calorie foods led to an increase in obesity with its resultant high blood pressure, cholesterol abnormalities, diabetes, and cardiovascular disease. Fast automobiles helped make accidents the number five most common cause of death and accounted for almost a million injuries on the roads and highways each year.

The treatment-oriented healthcare system stepped in to pick up the pieces as people began taking less responsibility for their own health. Many said we had the best medical treatment system in the world—and we needed it. We were developing into one of the least healthy populations among the industrialized nations and were spending almost twice as much per person as the next most expensive country. Today, we rank only twenty-fourth in "disability-adjusted life expectancy" among the member states of the United Nations.

The tales begin in 1959 when an explosive era of technological medical innovations was just beginning. The first antibiotics had been introduced only fifteen years before, and a burgeoning number of newer and more effective ones were appearing almost on a monthly basis. The first open-heart surgery was performed in 1952 to close a hole between heart chambers, but surgery for coronary artery disease was still a few years away. Inventions, such as cardiac defibrillators, EKG monitors, CPR (cardiopulmonary resuscitation), ventilators for mechanically assisting breathing, and the use of intravenous drugs for controlling heart rhythm appeared in the medical journals just before 1960 and formed the foundation for developing intensive care units and emergency departments, but they would still require a few years to perfect.

The first two tales describe two of my medical professors, each dynamic in his own way, who demonstrate completely different points of view about the roles of physicians and the future direction of medicine. They contrast the efficiency of prevention with a growing emphasis on treatment of diseases that could have been avoided. One is engaged in the prevention and eradication of lethal epidemic diseases affecting huge numbers of underserved people around the world, while the other is an innovative orthopedic surgeon who repairs major traumatic injuries often arising from industrial and motor vehicle accidents.

The next two sketches recount events that occurred when I was a young physician serving as a flight surgeon in the United States Navy during the Vietnam era. The navy was still trying to learn about unexpected health consequences associated with high-performance jet aircraft operating from carriers and spent substantial amounts of money training physicians to observe and to help build a body of knowledge that became the specialty of aviation medicine. Ironically, for limited periods of time those flight surgeons were the family doctors for surrogate families of tightly bonded members of carrier squadrons during times of high stress, and as such, those squadrons resembled somewhat the true families and communities of an earlier era. Flight crews not only cared for each other, they were willing to die for each other as well, and many of them did.

Other tales relate my experiences and those of my colleagues in the late 1960s and early 1970s while we were learning new specialties in the now high-tech hospitals with their emphasis on advanced, complex, multisystem diseases. We were fascinated with our work and exhausted by the long nights helping to save the lives of patients who were sicker than any who had survived in prior decades. For a time, new procedures raced ahead of the necessary training, so a small number of physicians carried a heavy load.

Some of the tales are character sketches that describe colleagues and patients. Through all of the scientific and technological changes in medicine, close human interactions often remained, although irrevocably different. The tales reflect the hopes, fears, and frustrations with the current healthcare system that all of us feel.

The last two tales, "The World Series Was Postponed Today" and the fictional short story "Influenza," look at groups of people isolated in their own world, but coming together during a stressful event and acting for the good of the community, a throwback to an earlier time. The first recounts a real natural disaster, and the short story, "Influenza," describes a recent real disease outbreak that occurred in Asia, but that I transformed into a fictional American event. They describe a cultural phenomenon where strangers transcend their own self-centered interests and begin to care about each other and to work together for a common cause. The people experiencing these events contrast with television viewers who impassively watch the disasters as a sort of entertainment, like rubberneckers staring at the crumpled remains of an automobile accident.

I did not intend *Doctor Tales* to be a history of medicine in the twentieth century, but rather, only quick snapshots of important issues through the eyes of one physician who lived through the changes. Some of the stories shed a ray of hope; others don't. The unfolding adventure of medical advances continues, but by looking at where we've been, we might make better decisions about our future directions. I have arranged the tales chronologically beginning with the thoughts of an impressionable first-year medical student.

Tough Tony DePaul

Every morning Tough Tony DePaul put on a red tie, a perfectly ironed blue shirt, and a perfectly pressed blue suit. He permitted no excess fat on his wiry five-feet-eight-inch frame, and he looked like a marine gunnery sergeant in dress blues ready for inspection. At exactly the same time every day he would stride to the hospital, stopping first at the same barber shop to receive the same shoe shine from the same bootblack. The men in the shop always greeted him with a respect that bordered on veneration.

"Good mornin', Doctor. Your chair is waitin' on you."

"Good morning, Leroy. It's going to be another hot one."

"Yessir, I believe so, Doctor. It's goin' to be mighty hot."

Philadelphia suffered brutally hot weather in the summer and frigid temperatures in the winter. On summer afternoons, the sun baked the canyons of concrete and asphalt, magnifying the heat and humidity, and emptying the sidewalks of pedestrians. Uncollected garbage ripened quickly, emitting a pungent odor that permeated into the hospital. Air conditioning had not yet arrived, at least not in any parts of the hospital that patients occupied, and certainly in none of the spaces dedicated to medical students. In the operating rooms, one medical student would always be assigned to mop the brows of the surgeons and nurses who were "scrubbed in" to prevent dripping onto the operative field. Student nurses on the wards kept the windows open in hopes of catching any breeze, but they also caught the fine rain of soot that powdered every surface. When a nurse made a bed at ten o'clock in the morning, it would display a layer of fine black ash by two o'clock.

The hospital was located between the venerable nineteenth-century Academy of Music, home of the famous Philadelphia Orchestra, and Independence Hall, home of the Liberty Bell. Nearby stood the stately brick houses and sycamore trees of Clinton Street and the high-rise office buildings of Chestnut Street, but the slums of South Street festered not far away, too. Forgotten neighborhoods were lined with derelict Father-Son-and-Holy-Ghost houses, small three-story, three-room houses with one room on top of the other. Many of them would soon be bulldozed to make way for the expanding "Society Hill." Philadelphia was trying to recall the glory days when the nation's founders had signed the Declaration of Independence, but most of the residents at that time were not part of high society.

With his gleaming black shoes, Dr. DePaul would continue on his way, taking care to avoid stepping on the homeless people sleeping on the sidewalk during the only tolerable part of the day. Those poor people exhibited an astonishing variety of advanced diseases that we medical students would see only rarely in our future practices: tetanus, diphtheria, rickets, beriberi, tuberculosis of bone, Wernicke's alcoholic encephalopathy, and one with a syphilitic thoracic aortic aneurysm. We can easily prevent every one of those diseases, but once they are established, the victim enters a horrible nightmare.

The neighborhood endured plenty of crime, but anyone associated with Jefferson Hospital was off-limits to petty criminals who never knew when they would need us as a result of their high-risk activities. Since our neighbors couldn't tell us apart, they treated anyone wearing a white coat as a celebrity, even lowly first-year medical students.

"Good mornin', doc. God bless ya."

But our privileged social status disappeared immediately upon entering the wards; nursing students and orderlies looked us over with justified suspicion and contempt. One lone senior student nurse had charge of each long open ward of thirty patients, all very sick, and she had no time for novice medical students coming in to see our first patients.

"Don't stand around staring like a bumpkin. Help me clean up this patient and move him into a chair. Then you can examine him."

White iron beds with the feet toward the long center aisle lined the walls making two rows, like in a military barracks. The sheets were white, the blankets were white, the chairs were white, and the walls were white. Large windows along one wall had no curtains and were always kept open in summer. The student nurse in charge of the ward had a desk in the center of one of the rows, but she never had time to sit there, because the patients were far too sick. She gave each patient a rank: the sickest toward the center of the ward, alongside and across from her desk, and the less sick farther away toward the two end walls. Curtains hung from an overhead track around several of the beds toward the center, but they were pulled back most of the time.

It was when they were not pulled back that the nurse was busiest. Behind the curtains a patient would be moaning, or screaming, or bleeding, or desperately short of breath, or dying. In those situations, first-year medical students could do little except to become assistants to the student nurse. Cardiopulmonary resuscitation, or CPR, had just been invented, only we called it "mouth-to-mouth resuscitation" and "closed-chest massage." We weren't yet very good at it, and many of our patients would have been better off without it. Doctors and nurses had not yet become as skilled in prolonging the act of dying as we would later.

At the hospital, Tough Tony put on a fresh, perfectly ironed, long white coat that bore the label "Dr. DePaul, Chief, Orthopedic Surgery," and then headed for the amphitheater that had served as an operating room during the nineteenth century. This historical landmark appears in the famous Thomas Eakins painting in the main foyer of the medical school, intimidating every new medical student on his first day at Jefferson Medical College.

The painting, called "The Gross Clinic," 1875, measures eight feet by six and a half feet, and shows the celebrated Samuel Gross operating on a patient's leg. There are no gowns or gloves or masks or drapes, and no anesthesiologist. The famous surgeon in his black coat apparently had no regard for the antiseptic technique that Joseph Lister had introduced ten years earlier, or for the use of anesthesia first introduced forty years earlier. The students on the banks of benches surrounding the center of the amphitheater are frozen, leaning over in rapt attention watching the operation. In the dark mud background of the painting out of the bright light on the patient, a woman, possibly a mother or a wife, holds her open hand to her forehead in horror.

In the mid-twentieth century, that same amphitheater served only as a lecture hall, but the students were still arranged in the same tiered rows around the operating "theater," and still felt the same anticipation and stared with the same fascination as soon as the professor entered the arena. Dr. DePaul was the lead actor and appeared with his starched white coat, red tie, and shiny shoes, making no compromise with the stifling heat.

Immediately, an orthopedic surgery resident began presenting a case and interpreting the X-rays while an orderly wheeled in the patient, a young woman, very thin and bent over guarding her right shoulder. Several years before, she had suffered major trauma to her shoulder and upper arm that resulted in an angulated and frozen joint. She appeared anxious in the bright lights under the stares of an army of male medical students.

Dr. DePaul approached her.

"Miss, would you mind removing the top part of your gown so that everyone could see the deformity?"

She looked terrified. He began his discussion, not stopping to listen for an answer.

Reluctantly she complied, awed by Dr. DePaul's presence.

He took hold of her arm. "This doesn't hurt, does it?"

She grimaced, barely able to suppress a scream. The scene resembled the one in "The Gross Clinic."

He pointed to her shoulder. "Tomorrow, we're going to make an incision from here over to there, and then we're going to release the frozen joint and saw the bone here. We'll put in two screws like this one to stabilize the humerus."

The patient anxiously regarded the screw, which looked like a fastener that might have been used in a garden furniture factory.

All of the medical students squirmed because of the embarrassment that the patient was suffering, but at the same time, all knew they were in the presence of one of the gods of orthopedic surgery. Few surgeons in the world had the capability to perform this kind of reconstruction. The operation that the patient would undergo the next day would be the best chance that she would ever have to correct her painful deformity. Even if one of the orthopedic surgery residents performed the operation, Dr. DePaul would be in the operating room making sure that the procedure was done exactly right.

The patient replaced her gown, and the orderly wheeled her out. A different orderly, together with a student nurse, wheeled in the next patient in a bed rigged with an overhead frame. He had suffered a fractured femur in an industrial accident, and the orderly and nurse had temporarily dismantled his traction apparatus and rested his leg on pillows with a splint in order to transport him from one of the wards. He, too, appeared confused in the dazzling lights in front of the large audience. Dr. DePaul approached the bed.

"Good morning, Mr. Howard. We're going to show a group of doctors how your traction apparatus works."

Dr. DePaul put up the original X-rays showing the shattered bone, angulated at mid-thigh.

"Amputation would have been the only option prior to the twentieth century, but now we use six months of traction in bed, and then another three months in a long-leg cast."

In just a few minutes, Dr. DePaul reassembled the traction apparatus using a web of ropes, pulleys, and weights that resembled the rigging on a sailing ship. He carefully measured the angles and applied the weights, all the time explaining the importance of precision. Bed rest of that duration would cause a loss of both bone mass and muscle mass, but in the end, the patient would keep his leg, and he would be able to walk again.

Dr. DePaul then produced a "nail" that he declared would revolutionize the treatment of major fractures like the one that the patient had suffered. This nail was, in fact, a rod about a foot long that would be inserted into the bone marrow cavity through a hole drilled at the top of the femur at the hip. The surgeon could then pound the nail with a large mallet nearly the full length of the bone, so that the patient's thigh would be steel-reinforced. Later, manufacturers would substitute lighter-weight titanium for the steel. Patients with broken femurs could be walking again within days instead of lying in bed for six months. It sounded like science fiction, but nails revolutionized the recovery from femoral fractures.

When Dr. DePaul finished talking, an orthopedic surgery resident dismantled the traction apparatus and replaced the splint and pillows so that the orderly could transport the patient back to his ward.

The first orderly returned wheeling in a third patient, a white-haired woman with her left wrist badly deformed and her forearm immobilized with a splint and sling. She had fallen at home during the night on a trip to the bathroom and had come to the emergency department with a Colles' fracture, named for Abraham Colles, an Irish surgeon at the turn of the nineteenth century. That kind of fracture commonly occurs in older women who fall forward with arms outstretched, breaking and dislocating the end of the radius, a long forearm bone that forms a part of the wrist. A resident introduced her to Dr. DePaul.

"Good morning, Mrs. Grabowsky, how are you feeling?"

Mrs. Grabowsky mumbled something unintelligible, and Dr. DePaul continued to address the audience with a story about Dr. Colles and the frequency of this type of fracture, and at the same time, casually reached for the patient's wrist.

She eyed him with suspicion.

"We're just going to inject a little numbing medicine into your arm."

"Why? What are you going to do?"

He explained it all using anatomical and technical terms, all the time facing the audience in the amphitheater.

Mrs. Grabowsky began to shift uncomfortably.

"My arm feels just fine the way it is."

"Don't worry, this will only take a minute."

Before she could breathe another word, the needle was in her wrist, directly into the swollen area of the fracture. She grimaced and let out a little scream.

"There, that wasn't so bad, was it?"

Another orthopedic surgery resident, who had been standing unnoticed behind the wheelchair, gently wrapped his hands around the patient's upper arm and elbow. He apparently knew his role exactly. She twisted to look up at him.

"What are you doing?"

While she was looking away, Dr. DePaul picked up her hand and the two doctors began to pull on her forearm in opposite directions. She let out another little scream. Dr. DePaul continued to face the audience.

"This is called traction and countertraction. We've taken the pressure off the site of the fracture, and now watch how I can easily manipulate the broken end of the radius back into place."

The wrist was perfectly aligned. A technician all in white from the "cast room" had brought in a cart that he wheeled close to the patient. Without a word spoken, he began to apply a soft wrap to her forearm and then began dipping stiff strips of gauze impregnated with plaster of Paris into a basin of warm water. He expertly wrapped several layers of the now-pliant plaster strips and rubbed down the final layer as smooth as a Roman sculpture. The whole procedure from needle to plaster had consumed little more than five minutes.

"Each of you will be able to do this now when you have your own practice."

We looked doubtfully at each other as the orderly wheeled out the patient, who continued to stare at the plaster cast on her arm. Dr. DePaul was one of our heroes. He was a surgeon who did procedures instead of just talking about them.

Dr. DePaul had introduced an almost endless list of new techniques that modernized bone and joint surgery, and more importantly for us, he had compiled an up-to-date atlas of current procedures with beautiful sketches that facilitated and simplified our learning. His protégés were going to become the most advanced orthopedic surgeons of our era. Nevertheless, each medical student also learned something about empathy and compassionate care—or rather, what they were not in the bright lights of a surgical "theater." But the drama in that hallowed historical site affected us. Years later, we would all remember the patients, their injuries, the amphitheater, and Dr. DePaul.

I learned to reduce fractures, apply plaster casts, and assist in the operating room. When I became a senior medical student, I delighted in being directed to set up traction for a patient with a lower extremity fracture. On the wards, setting up ropes, pulleys, and weights at exactly the right angle and with exactly the right amount of tension, as shown in my DePaul atlas, gave me great pleasure. I also experienced a little fear knowing that Tough Tony would see my creation and render a loud opinion if it were not just right. In spite of Samuel Gross's contempt for infectious diseases, we all used Joseph Lister's antiseptic surgical techniques, and so we rarely saw a wound infection and never a postoperative fatality. Our results were superb from the viewpoint of function and form, although our patients certainly didn't enjoy the experience.

At the time, I didn't know that I would rarely use my new skills as a sawbones, because my future specialty would be internal medicine. However, my new knowledge about sprains, strains, and back pains, did come in handy. My future patients with their heart disease, strokes, diabetes, and emphysema suffered plenty of aches and pains, and occasionally, I found myself in a situation where a patient needed an emergency reduction of an acute dislocation.

A number of years later, my daughter Sarah applied to Jefferson and was accepted. I was proud. She traveled to Philadelphia for a visit and saw the famous Thomas Eakins painting and the dark mud portraits of distinguished nineteenth-century Jefferson physicians lining the corridors. Jefferson is the third-oldest medical school in the United States, founded in 1824, and I am among the more than twenty-seven thousand former students to have received medical degrees there. As a group, we make up more living graduates than from any other medical school in the country. One of my former professors at Jefferson, Dr. John Gibbon, Jr., invented the first heart-lung machine and performed the first open-heart surgery there in 1952. I had the opportunity to examine that patient ten years later.

But Sarah noticed that the first woman medical student was not admitted to Jefferson until 1961, and that no women appeared in any of the portraits. She wanted to become a pediatrician and have a close rapport with her patients and provide them with personalized care. "The Gross Clinic," open-heart surgery, and the legendary Dr. DePaul implied a different tradition.

Four other medical schools accepted Sarah, and I was a little sad that she decided not to attend Jefferson. She ultimately had four wonderful years as a medical student at another university where she learned a great deal about compassionate care. Today, she is a very successful pediatrician and adored by her patients, many of whom are young teenaged girls for whom Sarah is a role model. She never learned how to set up traction for a patient with a broken femur, but then nobody ever uses traction anymore anyway. Maybe it is more important for medical students to learn about people than about technical advances.

We all have our heroes, but I have to acknowledge that my hero Tough Tony DePaul was a relic of the nineteenth century. Maybe I am too. I worshipped Pasteur, Koch, Lister—and DePaul. Dr. Anthony DePaul represented a new breed of specialists whose expertise far surpassed their predecessors both in knowledge and skill, but the new breed was also the beginning of a decline in the rapport between physicians and patients. Sarah later showed me her interpretation of twenty-first-century medical education with its emphasis on establishing a long-term close relationship with her patients. Both her patients and her colleagues prefer Sarah's version.

KG

The word got around quickly about KG's suicide. We were all spread around the country involved in our busy practices, but enough of a network still existed that every member of our class knew within a few days. The news surprised none of us, but each was aware that a person who had significantly influenced our lives was now gone. He had lived alone, and as far as we could observe, he had no friends. We only knew him as students or had been aware of his research. First- or second-year students never approached him, and only those who had completed the basic sciences and were finishing the clinical years would dare.

Kenneth Goodner, PhD, terrorized first-year medical students. For the weekly oral exam, he arranged about seventy students in a semicircle and fired one do-or-die question at each student.

"Mr. Marlier, name one organism in the normal flora of the nasopharynx."

"Alpha streptococcus?"

"Right, that's four points."

KG wrote down a four in his roster next to the name Marlier.

"Mr. Beebe, the normal flora of the trachea contains which organisms?"

"Alpha streptococcus?"

"No!"

"Sir, I thought there weren't any bacteria in the trachea normally."

"So, why did you guess alpha streptococcus?"

"I answered too quickly."

"All right, but you only get a three instead of a four for a correct answer."

KG wrote down a three in his roster next to the name Beebe and then consulted his list for the next victim.

"Mr. Bentley, what does the name Lübeck mean to you?"

"He was a nineteenth-century microbiologist?"

"No! Lübeck isn't a he, it's a where."

KG wrote a zero next to the name "Bentley."

"Mr. Billings, perhaps you can inform us about Lübeck."

"It's a town in Germany?"

"Brilliant, Mr. Billings, but why would I ask you about a town in Germany?"

"I don't know, sir."

KG wrote down another zero, this time next to the name Billings.

"Lübeck, gentlemen, is the city where Robert Koch conducted his disastrous tuberculosis immunization experiments on 240 children. Almost all of them developed active tuberculosis and seventy-two died. As a result, Koch considered his life a failure, and he never worked again."

"Mr. Bissell, do we have a vaccine against tuberculosis today?"

"Yes, sir, BCG. But it provides only incomplete immunity and it eliminates the usefulness of tuberculosis skin testing as a diagnostic tool."

KG wrote down a four next to the name Bissel.

"Mr. Goldstein, what do the letters BCG stand for?"

"Three Frenchmen, but I can't remember their names."

KG wrote down a zero next to the name Goldstein.

"Mr. Goldstein, BCG stands for bacillus Calmette-Guérin, which is a weakened strain of *Mycobacterium bovis.* It causes tuberculosis in cows and can be transmitted to humans in cows' milk. Two Frenchmen, Albert Calmette and Camille Guérin, repeatedly subcultured *M. bovis* in artificial media until the organisms became weakened and no longer caused tuberculosis in either animals or humans. Injection into humans has provided partial immunity against human tuberculosis, and it has been given to more than two billion persons as a vaccine against tuberculosis in developing countries around the world. It has undoubtedly saved millions of lives, and is completely safe. However, public acceptance was slow initially because of the memory of Koch's disaster in Lübeck."

We had thoroughly studied current textbook microbiology, but KG was now quizzing us about what we considered to be arcane history from the nineteenth century. He argued that research on disease prevention was not nearly completed, and that enthusiasm for treatment with antibiotics would displace as passé nearly all research directed at prevention. Most of our improvement in longevity during the twentieth century was due to public health implementation of preventive concepts first developed by nineteenth-century scientists like Louis Pasteur, Robert Koch, and Joseph Lister. They had learned that we could prevent some infectious diseases through programs such as clean water and sewage treatment, more liberal use of soap and disinfectants, immunizations, refrigeration, and quarantine for contagious diseases like tuberculosis.

KG exalted in the rapid evolution of our understanding of infectious diseases during the late nineteenth century. In the eighteenth century, medicine had been mostly a cult with physicians using cure-alls like bleeding, purges, and leeches. Most people died young of infectious diseases, which physicians assumed were passed from person to person through odors and mists. In a breakthrough in 1799, Edward Jenner noted that milkmaids all acquired cowpox, but never developed smallpox. By intentionally exposing children to cowpox, he could prevent one of the most deadly pestilences of the time. However, most people rejected the revolutionary idea of what we now call vaccination, and widespread adoption would not take place for another one hundred years. Today, because of worldwide acceptance of smallpox vaccination, no country has reported a new case of smallpox since 1971.

A major turning point in preventing infectious disease occurred in 1857 with an article written by an obscure French chemist working in a laboratory of a consortium that was trying to discover the cause of wine spoilage, a serious economic problem in France. His name was Louis Pasteur, and he had observed through his microscope tiny living things that he called "microbes" that were present in spoiled wine, but absent in good wine.

L'Academie des sciences in Paris considered Pasteur's work to be a giant step forward for wine production, but others saw something much more. In one short phrase in the middle of his landmark article, Pasteur wrote that these same microbes might also cause infectious diseases. Years later, medical historians referred to the article as the origin of "the germ theory of disease." Pasteur had completely transformed our understanding of the causes of the most common diseases and had introduced the possibility of preventing them.

Soon after, surgeon Joseph Lister in Glasgow noted Pasteur's work and began experiments using harsh chemicals that we now call antiseptics. Wound infection following surgery killed a high percentage of patients, limiting surgery to use only as a desperate, high-risk last resort—for example, to interrupt the spread of gangrene after an accident or bullet wound. He divided surgical patients into two wards, one to undergo surgery using antiseptics and the other to receive standard care with no antisepsis. Without antiseptics, the mortality rate from wound infection remained high, but with Lister's new antiseptic techniques, the mortality rate dropped to zero. If not for Pasteur and Lister, surgery today would still be in the dark ages. Because of our understanding of microbiology we can safely and routinely do surgery not only in the abdomen, but even on the heart and brain, something that would have been completely impossible without antisepsis.

Work by both Louis Pasteur and Robert Koch led to the widespread use of quarantine for tuberculosis. It was so effective that tuberculosis declined from the most common cause of death in Europe and North America in the nineteenth century to only three deaths per one hundred thousand persons per year by the middle of the twentieth century—before the introduction of the first antibiotic for tuberculosis. Today, tuberculosis bacteria are often resistant to all antibiotics; the mortality rate is no better now than before antibiotics were introduced.

KG sometimes expressed regret about the development of antibiotics, because he believed that we would all become complacent and overconfident about having conquered infectious diseases, mistakenly thinking that we could effectively cure anything with the new wonder drugs.

Of course he was right. We nearly abandoned our efforts at developing new methods of prevention during the last half of the twentieth century, and by the twenty-first century, rapid evolution of resistance to antibiotics, and the high cost of bringing new antibiotics to market, severely curtailed their usefulness. For most worldwide epidemics today, antibiotics have either limited effect or no effect, as in the case of HIV/AIDS, hepatitis, malaria, typhoid fever, many diarrheal infections, and antibiotic-resistant tuberculosis. In parts of Africa, South Asia, and South America, life expectancy remains far below that of the industrialized nations, and public health precautions are only just now developing. KG insisted that all medical students be aware of the history of the struggle to prevent the tragedy that infectious diseases still cause in the lives of so many around the world.

To that end, KG traveled every year to Thailand for the dry season. When the amount of rainfall declines, the current in the rivers diminishes, and the water level drops. Large numbers of people live and work on boats in the rivers, and they use the water both for drinking and for carrying away sewage. During the monsoons, the large flow of water keeps the bacterial count low, but during the dry season, the stagnant water creates an ideal culture medium for bacterial growth, and an epidemic of cholera would explode on the people with a devastating effect as an annual pestilence that had recurred for centuries. Part of KG's research involved the details of the environmental conditions in Thailand; he measured bacterial counts, water temperature, speed of the current, boat population density, and many other factors.

Cholera kills its victims by causing diarrhea, vomiting, and profound dehydration. Antibiotics don't work, but many victims would recover if they were just given large volumes of intravenous fluids because the disease is self-limited. KG showed Thai doctors and nurses how to concoct homemade intravenous fluids, and he gave his own money to buy reusable bottles, tubing, and needles. At that time, Thai health officials could not even imagine that the word "disposable" might apply to medical supplies. They boiled and reused everything. People were dying for lack of a five-cent needle, new or used. KG saved more lives during his lifetime than all of my classmates saved put together.

Today, the worldwide mortality rate from cholera has significantly declined, in part due to KG's efforts. In Thailand, for instance, new public health programs for sewage treatment and water purification have sharply reduced the number of cholera victims. For those who acquire the disease, survival is almost guaranteed if they have access to rural medical clinics that can administer intravenous fluids. Without access to fluids and electrolytes, the mortality rate remains just as high as in prior centuries.

Back in Philadelphia, KG worked on a vaccine for cholera, but with very little success. Others were working on it, too, and eventually a pharmaceutical company produced a commercial vaccine that required administration every six months, but its effectiveness was disappointing, and many people entering high-risk areas today decline to receive the vaccine. Cholera epidemics still regularly recur around the world, but prevention keeps mortality rates low primarily through more attention to sewage treatment and purification of drinking water.

KG lived in an apartment building on Camac Street in Philadelphia only a block away from the medical center. Most of the other tenants were medical students, interns, or residents. The "street" was really only a narrow alley, typical of eighteenth-century Philadelphia, and wide enough for only one car. KG's apartment faced a piano bar frequented by transvestites, adding to the Bohemian flavor of the student-dominated neighborhood. Around the corner, the police had made an arrest of a notorious woman bank robber who made the front pages of *The Philadelphia Inquirer* and kept journalists excited for weeks.

KG mixed very little with the other tenants, but he was always polite, and on very rare occasions, he would talk to us in the stairwell. Once, he came home in the early morning hours unable to find his keys and fell asleep in the corridor outside his apartment. Senior students and residents were also likely to come in during the early morning hours, and we helped KG by picking his lock to let him in his apartment. Some of us noticed a flat affect that made us worry about depression. Apparently, that worry was well founded.

We could admire KG only from a distance, as if he were a ghost from the Pasteur Institute during the second half of the nineteenth century. Few of us ever grasp what is most important in our lives in the way that he could. Today we spend huge amounts of money and medical talent prolonging the act of dying for patients who wish that we wouldn't bother. KG spent pennies per person on the wholesale preservation of life.

The Hero

The fire truck sped down to the far end of the runway. Ten seconds later the telephone rang in the small hospital at the U.S. Naval Air Station, Guam. The squadron executive officer, better known as the XO, was calling to alert us that an incoming aircraft had an injured air crewman on board and would land in ten minutes. A hospital corpsman jumped into the seat behind the wheel of our ambulance, and I climbed in next to him. We headed for the runway.

Our ambulance served as a rolling hospital and looked like a big gray box on wheels. A person six feet tall could almost stand, but not quite. We could breathe for a patient using a bag and mask, and we could even place a tube in the trachea to create an airway. The ambulance carried an EKG monitor and cardiac defibrillator, and we could give intravenous fluids and administer the same drugs available in a well-stocked emergency department.

I began to imagine the possibilities that we might encounter with the injured air crewman. The hospital corpsman on duty who took the phone call was certain that the XO had said "injured," and not "sick." An occasional air crewman flying out of bases in Vietnam had come in with malaria, dysentery, or typhus, but they were sick, not injured or wounded. Guam was two thousand miles from Vietnam, so why didn't the pilot do an emergency landing earlier—in the Philippines, for instance? My squadron's planes had been flying over North Vietnam, but after a mission, they usually landed on the carrier or "in-country."

They rarely flew all the way back to Guam, and they would never chance a three-hour flight with a seriously injured crewman. He must have been injured during the last half of the flight, or else the pilot would have turned back. And what kind of injury would have caused the pilot to alert the station before landing? That alone indicated something serious.

I was a flight surgeon, and for the past few months, I had been attached to VAP-61, a squadron of carrier planes with support facilities on Guam. Almost all of the students in my medical school graduating class two years before had received draft notices to serve in the military during the Vietnam War. After one year of internship at a hospital in Philadelphia, I opted to volunteer for the School of Aviation Medicine in Pensacola, Florida, to receive six months of special medical training, and at the same time to undergo basic flight training in the navy's flight school. The navy had been launching high-performance jets from carriers for only a few years, and the training program for my generation of flight surgeons was designed to help us learn as much as possible about the hazards that aircrews faced as a kind of laboratory for the new specialty of aviation medicine.

Flight surgeons were not surgeons; the term was part of the salty jargon on which the navy thrived. The flight crews always called me "doc," never Lieutenant Beebe. We could handle most medical emergencies, do minor surgery, manage some fractures, and perform the one function that the aircrews dreaded: we could ground any airmen who we considered unsafe to fly. I worked part of the time on Guam, either at the small naval air station hospital or at the full-service naval hospital ten minutes away, and part of the time I was on deployment on the aircraft carrier USS Coral Sea or at air stations in the Philippines and in Vietnam. On this day, I was on duty at the naval air station where I had expected a quiet, uneventful day.

The XO was already standing at the end of the runway next to the fire truck and was talking to the tower on the radio. He was undistracted by my approach, and wore a frown while staring intently at a spot on the ground and listening to the air traffic controller. His khaki uniform was neatly pressed, despite the humid tropical weather, and was ornamented only with the silver oak leaves of a commander and the gold wings of a naval aviator.

"What happened?" I interrupted.

"It's an A3. A panel on the canopy blew out."

An A3 was the biggest jet aircraft on a carrier with a large canopy over the cockpit that enclosed its three crewmen. Because of its size, the canopy was constructed of a patchwork of thick Plexiglas panels, one of which must have blown out causing a sudden decompression. Our squadron's aircraft performed photo and infrared reconnaissance, and they flew some of the most dangerous missions in the Vietnam War, because they had to fly slowly at low altitude between the mountains to get their pictures. The ever-improving North Vietnamese antiaircraft gunners found our big, slow A3s to be easy targets, and we had already lost several aircraft and their crews. A fragment from an antiaircraft burst could have pierced a Plexiglas panel, but this panel blew outward. My thoughts shifted to the types of injuries that might result from a sudden decompression.

The XO finished talking on his radio and turned to me with the details. The A3 had just taken off from Guam and was heading back to the carrier. They were climbing up to their cruising altitude when the panel from the canopy blew out without any apparent cause. One of the crewmen, a photo technician, had just unbuckled his seat belt, and the sudden decompression sucked him outside the cabin. Luckily, one of his boots jammed between the instrument panel and the side of the cabin, trapping him half inside and half outside. Airspeed at the time of decompression was about four hundred nautical miles per hour, and the blast of icy air buffeted the upper half of his body against the outside of the aircraft.

"Did he have a parachute?" I asked.

"No parachute. It's in the seat pan, and he had just unbuckled, so he'd be dead now if his foot hadn't caught."

"Are the pilot and navigator all right?"

"Yeah, they were still buckled in. The pilot slowed the aircraft, and the navigator grabbed the photo tech's leg and pulled him back into the cabin. His flight helmet was gone. Ripped off by the air blast. He's unconscious, and his face is all swollen. They have an oxygen mask on him. They're descending now, and the aircraft will be below ten thousand feet soon. They'll be landing in about five minutes."

"Ask the tower to find out if the crewman is breathing."

A minute later the XO responded. "The navigator isn't sure about his breathing. He started CPR."

A small aisle separated the seats of the pilot and navigator and extended back to the photo technician's seat. They were able to stretch out the crewman in the aisle to administer first aid, but I wondered how long it had been since the navigator had attended a CPR refresher course. Flight crewmen often postponed attending classes; they never knew from one day to the next where they would land. Sometimes it was back on the ship, sometimes at Da Nang or Bien Hoa in Vietnam, sometimes at Cubi Point in the Philippines, and sometimes all the way back to Guam where the technologically advanced photo labs were located. Flight operations in the Gulf of Tonkin off Vietnam were complicated for many reasons, but especially for reconnaissance aircraft serving requests from many sources on the ground. The flight crews had plenty on their minds, and often spent hours planning for just a few minutes over a target. Flying at low altitude in the mountains is dangerous even without antiaircraft guns shooting at them.

It sounded like a bad head injury—possibly fatal. I radioed the main naval hospital from the ambulance to warn them that an unconscious crewman was coming in, probably not breathing, and that we had a resuscitation in progress. We would be able to breathe for him temporarily in the ambulance using a bag, but at the hospital, they could take over with a mechanical ventilator in the ICU using equipment that we didn't have at the small six-bed hospital at the air station.

I had never heard of a blowout of a canopy panel, and my mind wandered back to the accident. I asked XO if he had ever heard of one like this.

"Never."

The XO had flown more than one hundred fifty combat missions and was a U.S. Naval Academy graduate. A few years later he was to become an admiral. He just stared silently at the approach end of the runway, lost in his own thoughts about the crewman. Several of our friends from the squadron had been killed over North Vietnam, but this accident seemed stupid and unfair after all that the flight crews had been through.

I told the hospital corpsman that we would meet the aircraft on the runway as soon as it stopped rolling. He already knew. He had heard my conversation with the XO and had started checking our equipment in the ambulance. He was just nineteen years old, and this was only his third week on "the island," but he seemed competent. Navy hospital corpsmen received excellent training, so he would have attended many first-aid classes about the care of an unconscious victim. All navy hospital corpsmen knew the basic ABCs: airway, breathing, and circulation.

Meeting all emergency landings was routine for the station firemen, so it was comforting to have extra hands available to help lift the crewman into the ambulance. The landing would be in three minutes, and we all searched the sky at the approach end of the runway. Runways at airports for jets typically extend for almost two miles with an additional mile of clearing at either end to remove obstacles to low-flying aircraft. The airport was also wide enough to allow for taxiways, hangars, and parked aircraft. Even though much of Guam was a jungle, the naval air station with all of the trees removed resembled a desert with a fine layer of coral dust mixed with sand everywhere. The reflected heat and humidity on Guam in the middle of the day was suffocating, especially out in the open on a runway. We were sweating for two reasons: the heat and our fear for the air crewman. No one spoke as the plane touched down.

As the A3 rolled to a stop, the ambulance and fire truck raced over to meet it. We immediately noticed the missing canopy panel on the port side. The navigator lowered the injured crewman through the hatch in the bottom of the fuselage to the hands of the firemen below.

"He's still unconscious!"

"Let's get him into the ambulance quickly!"

Firemen and hospital corpsman snatched the crewman and placed him onto a stretcher in the back of the ambulance. I climbed in to begin a quick examination to establish whether or not he had a pulse and was breathing, but before I could even look at the patient, the doors were slammed shut and the ambulance lurched forward, accelerating rapidly and hurling me against the back doors. With siren screaming and lights flashing, the hospital corpsman driving the ambulance raced toward the naval hospital. I hadn't noticed his growing anxiety as the plane approached, and had not reminded him that we would first examine the crewman to determine whether we needed to continue CPR. If the crewman had not been breathing, I could have safely begun mechanical ventilation en route with a mask and bag. With breathing assured, excessive speed would have been unnecessary. The corpsman had never before participated in a real emergency, so my failure to reassure him and to review with him our priorities during the few minutes before the plane landed was a teachable opportunity lost.

The trip to the hospital from the runway normally takes about eight or ten minutes, but my hospital corpsman behind the wheel was determined to make it in less. We skidded around the several sharp turns in the road, and each time I was thrown from one side of the ambulance to the other. I had anticipated using a small collapsible seat next to the patient's stretcher, but there hadn't been any time to set it up. I used all of my strength to avoid careening against the stretcher or the side of the ambulance. I couldn't maintain my balance enough to even look at the patient and still didn't know whether or not he was breathing. After one sharp turn, I found myself on the floor with the patient on top of me. He probably weighed about two hundred pounds, plus his flight gear and boots, and so I was having trouble breathing too. The next sharp turn rolled him back onto the stretcher, and I could breathe again, but I gave up trying to move.

In the longest eight minutes of my life, the ambulance screeched to a halt at the entrance to the emergency department. Hands reached into the back of the ambulance, grabbed the patient, and rolled him into the hospital. Dazed, and almost as bruised as the patient, I pulled myself together and staggered after him into the hospital. There, two physicians were standing next to the stretcher talking to the patient—*talking to the patient! The patient was awake!*

"Good work," proclaimed one of the physicians. "You got him breathing again. He's fully conscious."

I was stupefied! The ride in the ambulance had been awful, and now the patient was not only breathing, but he was conscious—*and talking!* My fears about his dying or suffering brain damage evaporated, and an enormous relief poured over me. Apparently, the air crewman had suffered a concussion during the buffeting after the decompression but was now waking up. His face was swollen and bruised like that of a heavyweight boxer after fifteen rounds, but he looked otherwise unharmed. I tried to explain to the doctors and nurses in the emergency department about the wild ambulance ride, but they showed no interest in me. They were quizzing the crewman.

"Do you remember what happened?"

"No, what am I doing here?"

"Do you remember being in the airplane?"

"Yes, I remember taking off, but I can't remember after that."

"Where were you going?"

"Back to the ship."

They pointed to me. "Do you remember this doctor?"

"Sure, he's our flight surgeon, but I haven't seen him today."

"You stopped breathing, and he's the one who got you started again in the ambulance."

With no amount of persuading could I convince anyone that I had been completely helpless bouncing around in the back of the ambulance, and that the patient had regained consciousness spontaneously. He probably had never stopped breathing in the airplane, but in the scramble of the emergency, the navigator took no chances and started CPR on the unconscious crewman. Certainly the crewman had suffered blows to the head causing a concussion, and the lesser oxygen level at high altitude probably worsened his unconscious state, but most concussion victims wake up eventually. This time, the air crewman just happened to awaken during the ambulance ride, and everyone mistakenly thought my first aid had brought him around.

The corpsman and I were still on duty, and we had to return soon to the air station with our ambulance in case of another emergency. This time I was the driver—a very slow driver and still very shaken. When we arrived, a huge crowd was waiting for us led by the XO. They had already heard by radio that the crewman was alert and talking.

"Here comes the hero!"

"You saved him!"

I was bewildered. "I didn't do anything. I was rolling around in the back of the ambulance like a pinball."

"Listen to that modesty."

"All you did was save his life."

I didn't feel like a hero. We were just lucky about the good outcome. In this case, the hospital corpsman knew the classroom material regarding the evaluation and care of an unconscious patient, but facing a real emergency was different. As a team, we lacked the rapport and experience to act quickly and expertly, and to avoid impulsive actions that might compromise the care of a patient. I should have taken the few minutes available before the plane landed to review the procedure with him. Medical emergencies require teamwork. We weren't yet a good team, but we would be.

Down in the South China Sea

The loudspeaker blared: "Flight surgeon to the chopper, on the double!" Sailors working on the flight deck of the aircraft carrier USS Coral Sea turned, momentarily looking at each other, knowing that something was amiss. The ship had already finished flight operations for the day, so a call for the rescue helicopter was unusual; moreover, a call for a flight surgeon signaled something especially bad.

Aircraft from the USS Coral Sea flew sorties twelve hours per day from midnight to noon, and her sister ship nearby, the USS Midway, handled the flight operations from noon to midnight. Each carrier launched a rescue helicopter to hover continually in case of an accident while aircraft were landing on the ship, or in case a returning aircraft was too badly damaged to land. When that happened, the pilot would have to eject near the ship, and the helicopter would fish him out of the water. Helicopter crews knew the drill, and ordinarily there was no need for a flight surgeon.

I grabbed my flight helmet and ran to the helicopter already starting its rotors, and we immediately lifted off. As we roared out over the South China Sea, I could see whitecaps below caused by the high winds from the deteriorating weather.

"What's up?" I yelled into my microphone over the roar of the helicopter's jet engine.

The helicopter pilot yelled back into my earphones, "An A3 is going into the water. The pilot can't transfer fuel from the wing tanks into the main tank. A valve must be jammed. They'll have to bail out in about five minutes."

"Where are they going down?"

"They're about two hundred nautical miles from the ship and almost five hundred nautical miles from Cubi Point."

Cubi Point was our forward support air base at Subic Bay in the Philippines, and the carrier was sailing just off the coast of Vietnam, so the plane was going down right in the middle of the South China Sea. Reaching them in the helicopter would take almost an hour, and since it was late afternoon, we wouldn't have much light left to find them.

The A3 Sky Warrior performed photo reconnaissance and was the largest carrier jet in the fleet, ordinarily carrying a crew of three people: a pilot, a navigator, and a photo technician. It had the longest range of any carrier plane and could stay airborne for hours without refueling. In fact, the fleet used another version of the A3 as a tanker for in-flight refueling. The photo reconnaissance version had three fuel tanks, two in the wings and one in the fuselage. They were carrying plenty of fuel, but due to a mechanical failure, they couldn't access it.

"Who's the pilot?"

"Ed O'Brian. He has a navigator and a passenger, a civilian engineer from Douglas Aircraft. The civilian has no survival training."

"Where were they headed?"

"They took off from Cubi Point and were returning to the ship. The aircraft needed major maintenance, and they had flown to Cubi Point a few days ago."

Aircraft mechanics could perform more complete maintenance and repairs at Cubi Point than on the carrier, and the plane was now en route back to the USS Coral Sea. The photo technician wasn't needed, and so he had remained on the ship. And since there was an empty seat, the pilot and navigator were bringing with them a civilian engineer from the Douglas factory to look at a problem on another aircraft on the ship.

A3s were the only carrier jets that had no ejection seats, so the crew would have to bail out through an opening in the bottom of the aircraft like on an old World War II bomber. A civilian with no training must have been horrified at the prospect, especially with the bad weather conditions, but ditching the aircraft in the open sea was out of the question. An A3 lands at a speed of about 120 knots per hour, which in this heavy sea would be like hitting the side of a mountain. The civilian would have to jump with the pilot and navigator if he had any chance for survival.

Once in the water, each survivor would have to inflate the one-man raft attached to his seat pan and parachute, and then find the strength to climb into it. In a rough sea and high winds, successfully detaching the wet, tugging parachute, deploying the life raft, and pulling up out of the water and into the slippery, bobbing raft would challenge even the well-trained pilot and navigator. They would quickly become exhausted. We had to try to find them and fish them out of the water, and we had to do it quickly, because by the time we reached them, the sun would be setting. They had flares and dye markers, but no electronic locater. We knew their coordinates, but we would need a lot of luck.

After what seemed an interminable time in the air, we approached the location where they had gone down and began searching the horizon. Suddenly, we all saw the flare at the same time. We were elated. Finding a tiny speck like that in the middle of the ocean, and finding it quickly, took great navigating, but it was a miracle nonetheless. We hovered over the raft, which was rising and falling on the fifteen-foot waves, and lowered a line with our winch. The helicopter pilot knew exactly how to drag the line to the raft, but because of the huge waves, several minutes passed before the survivor could grasp it. But once in his hand, he quickly slipped into the harness, and the helicopter crewman hoisted him up. If the pilot had not succeeded in bringing the line to the survivor, we would have had to lower the helicopter crewman into the water to bring it to him, a maneuver more dangerous and more time-consuming. This time, the rescue succeeded just like in the textbook.

We pulled up the A3's navigator, Lieutenant JG (junior grade) David Andrews, the squadron's survival training officer and most physically fit member. He was exhausted and a little cold.

"Have you seen the others?"

We hadn't. "Did you see them in the water?"

He looked worried. "No, I pushed our passenger out first and then jumped. Commander O'Brian was going to follow, but I couldn't see him. The wind scattered our parachutes, and after I landed in the water, I couldn't see anything. Climbing into the raft in these waves and that high wind took all my strength, and then I was constantly afraid of capsizing."

We continued hovering, searching the immediate area in the dying light but saw nothing. Lieutenant Andrews stared anxiously into the blackening sea. He didn't need my services except for helping him out of his wet clothes and into some blankets. My only prescription was a cup of dreadful hot coffee, the navy's universal cure-all. He looked below intently while holding the cup in his hands, barely noticing it. We should easily have found Commander O'Brian and the civilian engineer near Lieutenant Andrew's raft, but we saw nothing. The sea was empty.

The helicopter pilot began yelling into our ear phones.

"There's an LST only about a half hour away. They're going to continue the search. We have just about enough fuel to stay here over the spot until it arrives. The ship has a reinforced deck to accept a helicopter, but we can't land on it in this weather. They're going to continue the search, but they want me to lower you down by the hoist, doc, in case the survivors are in bad shape."

I had never made a house call as a flight surgeon before and speculated that being lowered onto a rolling deck at night might be dangerous, but I gulped and responded, "I'll be ready."

Lieutenant Andrews wanted to go with me and asked the helicopter pilot to radio back to the carrier to request permission. The operations officer on the Coral Sea immediately responded denying the request. The navy needed to gather quickly all the information it could to learn about the incident; Lieutenant Andrews was their best source. I would be going to the LST alone.

LST stands for "landing ship, tank," but each of the crewmen would have told you that the real meaning was "long slow target." This one was LST-1122, the 1,122nd commissioned by the United States Navy and christened the USS San Joaquin County, no doubt with a bottle of champagne from the central valley of California. During World War II, the navy built lots of LSTs just like number 1122 for the big landing on the main islands of Japan that never happened. Twenty years later, this relic was still lumbering around the Pacific hauling cargo, this time returning empty from Vietnam to the Philippines.

The ship was long, 328 feet in length, but narrow with only a fifty-foot beam. It had a flat bottom and drew only 3.8 feet of water empty, so it could practically crawl up onto a beach to load or discharge its cargo in order to support an amphibious landing of marines. The ship empty rode especially high in the water, and in a heavy sea, it would roll from side to side and climb up a wave until the bow extended over the top, hanging in midair. Then the whole ship would crash down on the other side of the wave, submerging the bow momentarily as if it were going to dive to the bottom; but it would always bob back to the surface, hesitating a few seconds before repeating the cycle.

The helicopter pilot and crewman would have to time my landing perfectly between wave crests, and once on the deck, I would have about two seconds to shed the harness. The movement of the deck was like a high-speed elevator that could easily break my legs, or worse, and the interval between waves was only a few seconds. I had practiced with a harness, but never at night onto a pitching deck. Somehow I made it down, but trying to move about on that deck was even more dangerous than being lowered from the helicopter. I didn't see how we were going to find Commander O'Brian and the civilian engineer.

The ship carried spotlights, and the sailors did their best during the night, but we knew that we had no chance. At daylight, the winds were even stronger and the waves higher, but we continued the search for three more days.

Duty aboard an LST numbed the body and soul, so sailors off duty became experts at sleeping on this clumsy roller coaster. They would climb into a bunk and lash themselves in with long seat belts, then snore away through the monotonous plunging and rolling. Each member of the small crew had several jobs, but they all took a turn as cook, leading to some doubtful gastronomic experiences. One crewman proudly presented his lemon meringue pie, a great triumph coming out of an LST galley. But sadly, he had miscalculated the amount of corn starch, so the lemon custard had the consistency of tough foam rubber. The resourceful sailors used a butcher knife in order to cut it, but nobody requested a second slice.

Time dragged on the trip to the Philippines, and I wrote my report, which I knew many people would read, but there was nothing much for me to write. Commander O'Brian had flown more than two hundred reconnaissance missions in combat areas of Vietnam without incident, but his plane went down in the middle of the South China Sea on a routine flight from the Philippines back to the USS Coral Sea. A mechanical failure had prevented delivery of fuel to his engines, and as a result, three people had to bail out into the sea in rough weather;

one survived and two didn't. Ironically, the Douglas engineer on board could have fixed the problem if the aircraft had been able to land.

I flew back to Guam, and a few days later, all of the families of the aircrews living on the island attended a memorial service for Ed O'Brian. He had been my friend, and many of the people attending the service had been my patients. They all sang "The Navy Hymn," also known as "Pilgrim's Pride," and I could not hide my tears. Being a flight surgeon was a psychologically hazardous business.

The navy asked flight surgeons of that era to learn ways to improve the safety of operating high-performance jets from aircraft carriers. I noted that the one survivor of this tragedy was the navigator who was the most expert in safety and survival, and the most physically fit. Even so, the ordeal of bailing out and being battered for one hour in the high wind and high seas exhausted him. Commander O'Brian knew more about flying combat missions than almost any other naval aviator, but he had made little effort at staying physically fit. He probably had died exhausted in the high seas before our helicopter arrived. The civilian engineer who had received no training probably perished immediately.

In a little more than fifty years since Kitty Hawk, the navy had achieved the astonishing capability of launching and landing supersonic jet aircraft on a ship, but we lost two lives because of a faulty valve and inadequate fundamental survival preparedness and physical fitness.

Code Eight

In the middle of May 1967, the war in Vietnam was over for me. I was going to continue my training for three more years to become board-certified in internal medicine, but the program didn't begin until July 1, so I decided to visit family members on the East Coast. After my war experiences, I was restless and distracted, but my parents, brother, and sister were glad to see me and kind enough not to notice my agitation. While visiting my brother in New York City, I met one of his neighbors at the elevator landing in his apartment building. I was in civilian clothes, and she had no idea who I was. She had just been to an antiwar demonstration and was still carrying her "Get out of Vietnam" sign. She explained to me all about the monstrous actions of American servicemen in Vietnam. Perhaps she was right. I was depressed.

Families warmly greeted veterans returning from World War II with small celebrations, and neighbors often prepared banners and a picnic. Sometimes the mayor, or high school principle, or a clergyman gave a small speech, not only to recognize the service of the young soldier, but to reestablish the integrity of the community and begin the soldier's reintegration. But, by the time of the Vietnam War, our agrarian, small-town culture had already given way to urbanization, and families were spread around the country. Furthermore, the war embarrassed many people who had convinced themselves that American military action was only making worse the plight of an impoverished people.

Consequently, most Americans were in no mood to recognize anything or anyone associated with the war.

July was therapeutic. So many critically ill patients filled the hospital that no time could be spared for further brooding about the deaths of my former comrades. In the early 1960s, intensive care units, open-heart surgery, cardiac pacemakers, and kidney dialysis were all still experimental, but by 1967, they had all become standard care. When I was a medical student, the hospital had boasted four ICU beds; now, three years later, the hospital where I was completing my specialty training had twelve, and they were never enough. We had to juggle the patients, always looking to transfer the least critically ill patients out to a regular medical unit.

Many of the drugs we had used before Vietnam disappeared and were replaced by newer and better ones. Members of the attending staff, the new name for clinical professors, were only slightly older than me, because young physicians were the only ones with any hands-on experience with the rapid technical innovations that would ultimately lead to an explosion of new specialties. In the intensive care units, some patients who would have died in a hospital of an earlier vintage were now clinging tenuously to life—and some were now surviving.

The chief of medicine, Dr. Henry Sparks, oversaw all of the dynamic changes and shepherded the young physicians in a fatherly way, especially those of us who were returning from Vietnam. He was a friendly, tall, lanky Californian who had a passion for working through puzzling diagnostic problems. If we had a patient with a particularly obscure infectious disease, he'd pick up a piece of chalk at a blackboard and talk a group of us through the clinical evidence to come up with a diagnosis. A few years later, he would become the director of a tropical disease research unit in Africa, but now, if we had a patient with a tropical infection, he became animated.

"What clues should we look for in the patient's story to help find the right diagnosis?"

"Recurrent bouts of shaking chills? Mosquito exposure? Contact with lice or fleas? Contaminated food or water?"

"Right. We have to ask about all of that."

"Let's name the most likely causes of this patient's persistent fever."

"Malaria, dengue, typhus, hepatitis, typhoid fever?"

"Right. Any thing else?"

"Melioidosis?"

"Right. Let's not forget melioidosis."

"What about the physical findings and laboratory tests?"

In short order, we would have mapped out a plan to lead us to the correct diagnosis, but often the big problem would be treatment. Antibiotics did not affect many of the diseases we were seeing, and in other instances, we saw antibiotic resistance that prevented the drugs from working.

Henry had a particular interest in an extremely rare tropical bacterial infection called melioidosis, which he would always insist on mentioning in the list of diagnostic possibilities in any patient coming from a tropical area with a fever of unknown origin. Because of Henry's obsession, we learned all of the published details about the disease, and we always performed the appropriate tests knowing that Henry would be sure to ask. In no reported case had a victim ever survived, and some of us began to wonder if we had been reading about the microbe version of bigfoot.

However, late one night, I admitted a patient with a fever who had just arrived on a flight from Southeast Asia. He was an engineer who had been working on a government project in a remote area of Thailand for more than a year, and he was an alcoholic. Melioidosis was more likely to attack alcoholics because of their lowered resistance to infection. I did the necessary tests, and to my astonishment, slides of the patient's sputum showed sheets of bacteria that looked like the tiny red safety pins characteristic of melioidosis.

Henry always had a meeting first thing in the morning with the residents who had been on call to go over the patients admitted during the night. With complete deadpan, I presented the case as if it were just another routine admission.

"I admitted a middle-aged man with a fever and a history of alcoholism. Twenty-four hours ago, he left on a flight from Bangkok and arrived here in San Francisco just a couple of hours ago. The flight radioed ahead for an ambulance, and they brought him directly here. When I examined his sputum under the microscope, I saw some strange-looking red bacilli."

Henry began to smile, convinced that I was pulling his leg. He wasn't so sure the disease existed either, but when I showed him the slides he became really excited.

"This is the first time I've ever seen it. There's no doubt about it. The patient has melioidosis."

We treated the patient with what we called "industrial-strength" doses of four of the newer antibiotics most likely to work in that class of bacteria. In spite of the treatment, blood cultures remained positive with increasing numbers of organisms, and after several days the patient died with overwhelming sepsis. Henry was disappointed, but realistic about it.

"We all hate to lose a patient, but we have to realize that antibiotics work against a very small spectrum of bacteria, and for many infectious diseases, we have no effective treatment at all. We have to work harder on prevention."

The following week we presented the case to a standing-room-only conference of physicians from other hospitals in San Francisco, all wondering if this would be the first of a series or just an isolated case. I'm sure that many physicians in San Francisco began looking for melioidosis in all patients with a fever coming from tropical areas for several months after. No one ever found another case, and I never saw another during my many years in practice, but we all relearned that the advent of the antibiotic era did not signal the end of fatal infectious diseases.

Henry and I always got along well, because I had seen a large number of patients in Vietnam with malaria, dengue, typhus, hookworm, dysentery, and many other tropical diseases. In California, we would on rare occasions receive a patient with malaria off a flight that had come in from a tropical country, and the laboratory would call me to look at a slide, because none of the laboratory technologists in California had ever seen malaria. In Southeast Asia, we had cared for as many as sixty marines with malaria on a single ward, and we had thrown out the tropical infectious disease sections of standard medical textbooks, because the descriptions resembled very little the diseases we were seeing, and we found standard treatments to be useless. In the mid-1960s, the pills that the marines took to prevent malaria gave them almost no protection in the jungle. We had to experiment and write our own textbooks. The surgeons did too. They saw more trauma and gunshot wounds in a week in Vietnam than most surgeons ever see in a lifetime.

Every weekend, I made rounds on all my hospitalized patients and sometimes saw some for a colleague who needed time off. One of them had admitted a frail seventy-five-year-old woman with a low-grade fever of several days' duration, but with no apparent cause. I decided to look her over carefully, because older patients with a persistent fever of unknown cause worry me. She had a prominent red spot, called a petechia, on the inside of one of her lower eyelids. I knew that one of the causes might be a tiny embolism of bacteria coming from her heart valve as a result of a rare disease called infective endocarditis, an infection of the lining of the heart. Common predisposing causes included a prior history of heart surgery, congenital heart disease, rheumatic heart disease, and self-injection using dirty needles by drug addicts.

At that time, those situations did not apply to very many of our patients, but I asked her anyway. She remembered that when she was a child, a country doctor had told her parents that she had rheumatic fever, but she and they had forgotten about it. She had never experienced undue shortness of breath with exercise. No other doctor had ever told her about the presence of a heart murmur. She did indeed now have the murmur typical of a form of rheumatic heart disease, later confirmed on ultrasound. Heart murmurs usually sound louder in patients when they have a fever, so it was no surprise that it may have been missed over the years.

I checked the blood cultures that my colleague had ordered the day before, and was not surprised to learn that all of them were positive for alpha hemolytic streptococci, the most common cause of infective endocarditis. I thought it was all routine, because my medical school professors had lived through an era when rheumatic fever was common, and they had talked endlessly about infective endocarditis. On Monday morning, I presented the patient's case.

"I looked in on a seventy-five-year-old woman admitted late last week with a low-grade fever who developed a heart murmur and a petechia inside her lower lid. Her blood cultures are all positive for alpha strep. She thinks she may have had rheumatic fever as a child, and I got a cardiac ultrasound that confirms a mitral valve abnormality consistent with rheumatic heart disease. I put her in the

ICU on Saturday morning and started her on high-dose intravenous methicillin. Her temperature is almost normal now and she's resting comfortably."

I was about to move on to the next case when Henry stopped me.

"You mean to say that you have a patient with infective endocarditis?"

"It seemed fairly clear to me."

"I've been in practice for twenty years, and I've never seen a case. Let's go take a look at this right now."

The patient was amazed by the huge entourage that trailed up to her bed, but she smiled from all the attention and gave us her most charming front. The still-visible petechia had begun to fade, and in listening to her heart, we all imagined that we still heard the murmur in the absence of the fever, but I was never quite sure. Since we all knew about the cardiac ultrasound showing an abnormal heart valve, perhaps we were trying to fulfill our expectation of hearing a murmur.

We continued the large doses of intravenous antibiotics over several weeks and her fever never recurred. All of her blood cultures remained negative. She never developed any complications, such as congestive heart failure, and left the hospital in good spirits. No other patient with infective endocarditis was ever admitted to our hospital during my three years as a resident. I became a celebrity for making the diagnosis of a rare disease that I mistakenly thought was common. Sometimes it pays to listen to old country doctors and emeritus professors talk about the old days. The antibiotic era had sharply diminished the incidence of infective endocarditis and improved the outcome.

Another of Henry's obsessions with rare diseases was a hereditary metabolic disease called acute intermittent porphyria. Henry had read extensively about the disease and the European royal families whose interbreeding had perpetuated the illness. Playwright Alan Bennett dramatized the disease several years later in his play "The Madness of George III." A group of London physicians instructed actor Nigel Hawthorne so well that I though we ought to check him to be sure that he didn't really have the disease.

In relapses of acute intermittent porphyria, the victim's urine left standing for several hours will turn a purple color, which was enough to convince anyone in the privy chamber of the validity of the king's divine credentials. In Mr. Bennett's play, one of the king's advisers first discovers this strange metabolic phenomenon.

"The king pees purple!"

The other actors scurry around the stage marveling at the discovery and nodding to each other. Certainly, any contemporary British subject whose urine turns purple would have a strong case for claiming royal ancestry.

One night, I admitted a patient who had some vague, nonspecific symptoms that acute intermittent porphyria could have caused, but porphyria was far down the list of possibilities. Because of Henry, I tested the patient's urine, and to my amazement, it was positive, confirming the diagnosis of acute intermittent porphyria. I repeated my deadpan scene at morning report with Henry, announcing that I had admitted another routine case of acute intermittent porphyria. I knew Henry wasn't going to believe this one, so I had brought a sample of the patient's urine and some test tubes and chemicals to perform the laboratory test right on Henry's desk. Henry was ecstatic, and it led to the only genealogy search on a patient ever conducted at that hospital.

All we could ever learn is that, although the patient thought he had ancestors from Great Britain, none ever had any hint of royalty. We also learned that no one in Great Britain had the slightest interest in proving that an American working man might be related to the royal family. The patient's symptoms completely cleared and never recurred, at least for the year that I could follow him, and eventually I lost touch with him. We knew that about one-half of patients who inherit the metabolic defect have only mild symptoms, and possibly never any at all. My patient probably had suffered some mild, transient, viral gastrointestinal distress, and just happened to be a not-very-royal carrier of acute intermittent porphyria, but Henry and I still treated him like the lost king of England.

Night call usually kept the residents very busy. We couldn't stray far from the intensive care unit, because many of those patients were caught in a life and death struggle. I would occasionally spend thirty-six hours in a row there because of a single unstable patient. Sometimes a patient on another ward would have a cardiac arrest, and the loudspeakers would blast out a call for the cardiac arrest team and crash cart. In most hospitals, the typical signal is "code blue," but at that time, we used the term "code four" to disguise the meaning for any anxious visitors or patients who might worry, not that anyone could mistake the meaning in the urgency in the call operator's voice or the sound of running feet in the corridors.

During one especially busy night, one of my colleagues had just arrived at the bedside of a patient who, seconds before, had experienced a cardiac arrest. The resident was just beginning CPR when the hospital operator announced a second "code four" on a different ward. The resident yelled for the intern to continue the first CPR and ran to the second, which was on a different floor. Miraculously, both patients survived, but the resident looked haggard the following morning. Henry asked him how the night went.

"I had a code eight!"

"What's a code eight?"

"Two code fours at the same time."

From then on, whenever too many emergencies were breaking loose at once, we called it a "code eight." We could always count on a large number of very sick patients coming into the emergency department on weekends, so Friday and Saturday nights were automatic "codes eight." Whether someone is a doctor, nurse, fireman, policeman, or parent, the high adrenalin level of simultaneous emergencies challenges even those with the coolest head.

Henry's weekly grand rounds were major spectacles. Every doctor tried to attend, and many came from other hospitals. The term "grand rounds" had nothing to do with examining patients on the wards, but was a conference in a large auditorium that was always filled to overflowing. Henry insisted that the patient always be present, and that the attending physician discussing the case conduct an interview so that everyone in the audience could hear the patient's story firsthand. Henry wanted to make sure that we made a connection with the patient, and not just with the disease or the patient's organs as an abstraction. He also insisted that listening carefully to the patient's own words would help lead us to the correct diagnosis.

The conference would begin with the resident recounting the patient's history, physical examination, and laboratory results. A radiologist would project the X-rays and other imaging studies on a large screen and describe the findings, and then a pathologist would project any microbiology slides, blood smears, or biopsy slides. Finally, we would bring the patient onto the stage for the interview that an invited clinical expert would conduct.

For one of those conferences, Henry decided that we should present a patient with irritable bowel syndrome, also called spastic colitis, characterized by recurring severe abdominal pain. We were surprised because irritable bowel syndrome was common, and the cases for grand rounds were typically rare diseases so that large numbers of physicians would have the opportunity to learn something new. In addition, all of the laboratory tests, X-rays, and biopsies in irritable bowel syndrome are usually negative, so there isn't much to talk about.

Henry had selected a gastroenterologist who was a master at interviewing patients. He knew that, beyond just the answers to questions, the patient's facial expressions, affect, and body language often told much of the story. Patients with irritable bowel syndrome are very uncomfortable, and they often undergo large numbers of unnecessary and distressing colonoscopy examinations and imaging studies searching for other diseases. However, the physician skilled at drawing out the history can eliminate many of the excessive diagnostic procedures and move sooner to a treatment plan, beginning with avoidance of any of the long list of drugs known to cause a worsening of the symptoms.

Henry and the gastroenterologist then began a discussion of the dietary guidelines that might help reduce the spasm, notably a diet high in both soluble and insoluble fiber. Henry acted as the moderator keeping the dialogue on track. They moved on to a discussion of how to relieve anxiety, a problem that worsens all gastrointestinal diseases. The patient was a middle-aged woman who had suffered from irritable bowel syndrome since she had been a young girl, but after the conference, she said that it was the first time in her life that she really understood the disease. The same thing was true for many of the physicians in attendance, including me. Henry knew how to teach, and he also knew what needed to be taught.

Although Henry tried to keep all of us connected to the patient, and not just to the patient's disease, many pressures interfered with establishing a close and enduring doctor-patient relationship. During the Vietnam War, I had felt closely attached to my patients, who were the squadron's aircrews and their families on Guam. When airmen were lost in combat or went down at sea, I wasn't able to shake myself loose from the grief.

During my hospital training with Henry, we were seeing far sicker patients than were typical of the ones when I was a medical student or a flight surgeon, because new technologically advanced treatments kept critically ill patients alive. Those patients were almost always withdrawn, and sometimes heavily sedated or unconscious, so we couldn't establish rapport with them. We usually saw the patients only during their hospitalization, and perhaps for a few visits after, but then we lost contact with them. The practice of medicine was evolving to become less compassionate and more disease-oriented, and we were erecting barriers to protect ourselves from feeling too much empathy. Very sick patients sometimes died, and we knew that becoming too attached would lead to early burnout. The price of becoming a hospital-based specialist was learning to focus on diseases while distancing ourselves from the patients themselves. Most of us didn't feel comfortable with the transition.

Night Call

Her pager went off three times within five minutes. The nursing station at one of the general medical units wanted her, the emergency department rang next, and then the intensive care unit. She chose to call the ICU first, because the condition of critically ill patients could deteriorate quickly.

"This is Dr. Collins."

"Mr. Davis is bucking against the mechanical ventilator, and the respiratory therapist can't adjust it."

Sixty-five-year-old George Davis suffered from chronic obstructive pulmonary disease, otherwise known as COPD or emphysema, and had been admitted to the hospital earlier that day in acute respiratory distress. The admitting resident had inserted a tube into the patient's trachea and placed him on a mechanical ventilator to assist his breathing. Mechanical ventilators resemble home washing machines, but with dials and gauges on the top and a bellows with hoses that lead to the patient. They make a noise like a wheezing giant sleeping. Everything had gone well for several hours, but Mr. Smith was becoming confused and agitated and began fighting against the mechanical ventilator. Dr. Collins wanted to check the oxygen and carbon dioxide level in the patient's blood to see if the problem was serious.

"Ask the respiratory therapist to get a set of arterial blood gases, and I'll be right there."

Then Dr. Collins called the emergency department and a nurse answered.

"Just a minute, Dr. Fallon wants to talk to you about a patient."

She could hear the nurse calling Dr. Fallon to the phone.

"I've got a sixty-two-year-old man here named Clarence Delaney with persistent chest pain for the last two hours, and with a blood pressure of 100 over 60 and a pulse of 130 beats per minute. He has a history of two prior heart attacks, and he's a two-pack-a-day smoker. He brought a bag with about six different drugs that he takes. His EKG shows an acute inferior myocardial infarction, and there's a portable chest X-ray pending. All of the lab work has been drawn, and we've given him ten milligrams of morphine. He's all yours."

An inferior myocardial infarction means injury, and maybe death, of a portion of heart muscle in the right ventricle. The heart tilts to the left side, so that the right ventricle is actually on the bottom, referred to as the inferior side anatomically. When a clot forms in the right coronary artery interrupting the blood supply, the acute lack of oxygen starves the heart muscle of the right ventricle. Damage to the muscle begins after only a few minutes. Inferior myocardial infarctions are dangerous, but generally not quite as lethal as anterior myocardial infarctions that affect the left ventricle, but in this case, the low blood pressure was a bad sign.

"Get the nurse to call admitting and I'll be right there."

Dr. Collins detoured to the ICU before heading to the emergency department. She quickly looked at the spreadsheet of data outside the patient's cubicle, ordered some adjustments to the mechanical ventilator settings, and increased the rate of intravenous infusion of a drug intended to dilate the patient's airways. Then she rushed to the emergency room. She had forgotten all about the call from the nursing station at the general medical unit.

Mr. Delaney was still grimacing from chest pain and his blood pressure had fallen further to ninety over forty. She looked at the nurse.

"Give me a syringe with twenty-five milligrams of morphine and set up a nitroglycerin drip."

She began injecting small doses of morphine into the IV tubing every two or three minutes, and gradually the grimace began to disappear. The nurse hooked up an IV bag containing nitroglycerin to the IV tubing.

"Start it at ten micrograms per minute."

The patient was beginning to relax, and his blood pressure came back up slightly to one hundred over sixty again. Dr. Collins began rifling through the patient's bag of drugs. His medication indicated that he had type 2 diabetes mellitus, angina pectoris, and mild high blood pressure. There was certainly no high blood pressure now. The weakened state of his heart muscle could no longer support the demands of his high pressure vascular system. She called the cardiologist on call.

"I've got a sixty-two-year-old man with an acute inferior myocardial infarction and persistent chest pain that began about two hours ago. He's in shock right now with a blood pressure down around ninety over fifty. Ordinarily, he takes medicine for high blood pressure. I'm giving him IV morphine at frequent intervals and have started a nitroglycerin drip. Should we try either a clot-dissolving drug or emergency balloon angioplasty?"

"He sounds unstable, and the myocardial infarction is already more than two hours old. It would take us too much time to set up for an emergency balloon angioplasty, so I'd use a thrombolytic drug immediately, like tPA. If you can clear the clot with the drug, we could consider him for balloon angioplasty tomorrow."

A cardiologist can insert a catheter containing an inflatable balloon into a narrowed section of a coronary artery in the heart and then inflate the balloon to mechanically dilate the artery and restore normal blood flow. Angioplasty is a procedure to change the physical structure of a blood vessel, by dilating in this case.

While they were talking, the monitor showed the patient's pulse dropping from 130 beats per minute down to 30. The patient paled and exhibited an awful aura of anxiety. Dr. Collins dropped the phone.

"I want one milligram of atropine stat!"

Dr. Collins inserted the syringe into the IV tubing and pushed the plunger. Miraculously the patient's pulse rose back up to 110 beats per minute, and his color improved. She picked up the phone again.

"Are you still there?"

"Yes, what happened?"

"The patient developed a profound bradycardia with a pulse down to thirty, and I thought we were going to lose him. I gave him some atropine and his pulse came back up."

Patients with inferior myocardial infarctions often develop a potentially lethal imbalance where their parasympathetic nervous system dramatically slows the heart by overriding the adrenaline of their overworked sympathetic nervous system. Atropine blocks the parasympathetic nervous system and allows the adrenaline to take over again to continue to drive the heart to maintain at least a minimum life-supporting function. Before the invention of electronic heart rate monitors, doctors and nurses had no way to detect such sudden slowing of the rate in time, and patients died.

"You'd better give him the tPA right away to see if you can open that artery."

"I'll do it immediately, and then I'll take him up to the coronary care unit."

The nurse placed the portable monitor and defibrillator on the gurney with the patient, and she and Dr. Collins took the patient up to the coronary care unit together. The patient's chest pain had gone, possibly from the morphine and nitroglycerin, and possibly because the tPA had opened the blocked coronary artery, but in any case, Mr. Delaney looked a little better. His blood pressure was still only 100 over 50, but his pulse was steady at 110 beats per minute, and he hadn't developed any major heart rhythm disturbance.

Her pager had gone off twice since the trip from the emergency department. The ICU was calling her again, and also the general medical unit that she had forgotten wanted her. She called the ICU first.

"Mr. Davis is worse. He's still bucking against the mechanical ventilator and he's extremely anxious. His blood gases show that his arterial oxygen level is falling and his carbon dioxide level is rising."

"I'll be right there. Is the respiratory therapist still in the unit?"

"Yes, he's here."

"Good, I want to ask him if he has any suggestions."

When she entered the ICU, she could see two nurses and the respiratory therapist huddling at the entrance to Mr. Davis's cubicle. The patient was soaked with sweat and would soon become exhausted. Dr. Collins was at a loss as to what to do next and looked at the respiratory therapist.

"What do you think?"

"I'd put him to sleep and take over control of his breathing with the ventilator."

She called the intensivist who was backing up the residents in the ICU.

"You've got to knock him out and take complete control of his breathing with the mechanical ventilator. It's just as if you had the patient under anesthesia. Give him short-acting narcotics and sedatives until he's asleep and put him on continuous mandatory ventilation. If he stays awake, he'll keep fighting the ventilator until he's exhausted, and then he'll stop breathing altogether."

Continuous mandatory ventilation means that the ventilator completely controls the rate of breathing and volume of air for each breath. Up to now, the mechanical ventilator had only assisted the patient by sensing when he was trying to take a breath, and then giving him a boost of air. But he was becoming erratic with his breathing efforts, and machine and patient were fighting with each other.

Ten minutes later, the patient was asleep. The mechanical ventilator was working smoothly and the patient's blood gases were already beginning to improve. The two nurses and the respiratory therapist looked a lot better too. The general medical unit paged Dr. Collins a third time, and this time she answered.

"Sorry, things have been a little dicey."

"We have an eighty-two-year-old woman admitted here this afternoon from a nursing home with pneumonia. She was alert when she was admitted, but now she's completely disoriented and screaming. We need you!"

"I'll be right there."

The abbreviated chart from the nursing home indicated that the patient had suffered a mild stroke several weeks before, but they had kept her in bed for fear of her falling. Each night they had given her a strong sedative so that she would sleep all night. The admitting physician had not wanted to suppress her breathing because of the pneumonia and had declined to order any more sedatives. The nurses on the unit were begging Dr. Collins to order a sedative because the patient was so disruptive.

"All right, I'll order it for tonight because she'll exhaust herself and everyone else on the unit, but we'll have to develop a plan for detoxification. She's probably undergoing drug withdrawal and might also have a little underlying dementia."

The older woman with her pneumonia and Mr. Davis in the ICU did get some rest that night, but Dr. Collins got no sleep, nor did Mr. Delaney in the coronary care unit. The anxiety from having a third heart attack, plus all the activity and noise, kept him awake despite the sedating medication that the nurse had given him. Dr. Collins admitted three more patients from the emergency department during the night, although none were as critically ill as either Mr. Delaney or Mr. Davis.

One patient was experiencing chest pain that lasted less than a minute, but it was recurring frequently with just minimal exertion. She admitted him to the coronary care unit for observation and called a cardiologist to consider the patient for cardiac catheterization in the morning.

Another patient was a young woman who had swallowed an entire bottle of tranquilizers as a suicide gesture. The nurses recovered most of the tranquilizers by irrigating through a tube that Dr. Collins placed through the patient's nose to her stomach. The patient was breathing normally, but Dr. Collins planned to keep the patient under observation until she became fully alert and a psychiatrist could evaluate her.

Toward dawn, the police brought in a young man who was hallucinating and combative after taking cocaine. Dr. Collins admitted him to the hospital for detoxification, and then went off to morning rounds where she presented her cases from the night to the attending physician and the other residents in her group.

"Mr. Davis is still unconscious under heavy sedation on continuous mandatory mechanical ventilation. I haven't tried to reduce the drugs to let him breathe on his own with just ventilator assistance. He was pretty exhausted when we took over his breathing for him during the night. We may want to keep him unconscious and do the breathing work for him for another twenty-four hours."

"Mr. Delaney has had no further chest pain, but his blood pressure is still a little low. I listened to his heart a few minutes ago; he has a gallop and some rales in his chest, so he's developed congestive heart failure. I've started to taper off the nitroglycerin drip. His heart rate remains about 110 beats per minute, and he's had no further episodes of a drop in heart rate, nor has he had any serious heart rhythm disturbance. His cardiac enzymes are markedly elevated, so he's had a major heart attack this time. I think he's pretty worried."

Mr. Delaney's weakened heart can't maintain his previous high blood pressure, and it also can't accept the high volume of blood returning to his heart. As a result, fluid backs up in his tissues, called edema. "Rales" comes from the French word râles that means noise, and in this case it refers to the sound in the lungs that the excess fluid causes with each breath. Dr. Collins also hears the typical gallop rhythm that a failing heart makes in trying to keep up with the body's demands.

Mr. Delaney survived to leave the hospital, but had severe congestive heart failure. He spent most of his days and nights in a recliner chair because of marked shortness of breath caused by persistent fluid in his lungs. If he tried to lie flat, the fluid would cause a suffocating feeling. His wife helped him with dressing and undressing, preparing his food, and aiding him to get to the bathroom with a walker. During weekdays while she worked, a caregiver came to help him. He died suddenly at home about six months after his hospitalization.

Mr. Davis recovered from his acute respiratory failure, and the doctors weaned him from the mechanical ventilator and removed the tube from his trachea. He was eventually discharged from the hospital, but had to use a portable oxygen tank, along with multiple inhalers and pills for his breathing. His family discovered that he was sneaking cigarettes from time to time. Over the following year, he was hospitalized three more times, but he died during a trip to the hospital in the ambulance a fourth time.

The elderly woman survived her pneumonia, and before leaving the hospital, she was weaned off all sedatives. However, she still exhibited slight dementia even off all sedating medication and remained confused at night. After she returned to the nursing home, the nurses persuaded a physician to reorder the sedating medicine. The doctors at the hospital never received a progress report and lost contact with the patient.

Dr. Collins was married during the last year of her training and delivered her first child two years after finishing her residency. She could not reconcile the conflicting needs of her newborn and those of critically ill hospitalized patients, so she took six months' leave of absence from practicing medicine. When she returned, she joined a group of hospital-based physicians who shared a practice that allowed her more time with her child. However, she later asserted that her first year back, juggling a young child and a busy practice left her more exhausted than any other year of her life.

Elliot Community Hospital Doesn't Exist Anymore

Mrs. Marion Putnam had lived all of her eighty-six years in the same town and in the same house on the same small farm as had her father, her grandfather, and her great-grandfather. A fireplace took up one whole wall of the house and was where her ancestors had cooked their meals and warmed themselves during the frigid New Hampshire winters. She liked showing visitors the hollowed stone where generations of Putnams had cracked walnuts and pointed out the heavy beams hewn by hand. Marion was born in that house, because in the nineteenth century, doctors in her town delivered all babies at home. Elliot Community Hospital was not to open until 1892, six years later.

Her husband had died and left her with little money, and her son had a good job in Boston, so she lived alone busying herself growing vegetables, raising chickens, and making her own clothes. A handyman lived rent-free in a small room in the barn and did chores in exchange for lodging and food from the farm. She drove an old car, but she didn't drive it often and not very far. She was well educated with a degree from Smith College, and she participated in two book groups and did volunteer work at both the Unitarian Church and the Elliot Community Hospital. Everyone in town respected her.

Her father had owned a factory in town, but she didn't own the small family farm; it belonged to her younger brother's daughter.

Her father never liked Marion and called her "brontosaurus" because she was six feet tall and a little awkward. Her mother had suffered a difficult delivery, and as a result, her father always blamed Marion for an obstetrical injury to her mother, as if being born were an unforgivable offense. The delivery also permanently damaged nerves in Marion's left shoulder leaving her with a withered arm.

When her father died, he left all of his estate to Marion's younger brother, including the factory and the farm. Her brother had preferred to live in town closer to the factory, and had allowed Marion and her husband, still living at the time, to continue to live on the farm. During the early twentieth century, manufacturing had declined in New England, so the factory closed, and ultimately her brother died. The farm then passed to her sister-in-law and subsequently to her niece, both of whom preferred to live in the bigger and more modern house in town. Not knowing what to do with either old Mrs. Putnam or the old farmhouse, the niece allowed Marion to continue to live there as a sort of caretaker.

Marion's health had been robust all of her life in spite of her withered arm, and she relished living close to the earth. She "put up" her garden vegetables in glass jars for the winter and made cider from the apples in her centuries-old orchard. She held dear the way of life of rural New England and loved cracking jokes about it.

"We have two seasons in New Hampshire: winter and the Fourth of July."

"In New England, hardship is a virtue."

"New York? You can't get there from here."

She loved to tell stories to the children who lived nearby and who would come to visit and to listen. Sometimes the old woman would read to them *Just So Stories* of Rudyard Kipling, or parts of Kenneth Grahame's *The Wind in the Willows,* and they would look intently at the pictures. In the summer, the children would make a tour of the vegetable garden, the chicken pen, two goats, and then play in the barn. On Halloween, they came in costume, and she would always have candy ready for them.

One year as she was reaching for her basket of candy, she tripped on a rug and fell into a doorway knocking her head, breaking her glasses, and badly cutting her face. The children were horrified and ran for help. The handyman and the children's mother took Marion to the hospital in the old car and called her niece in town and her son in Boston to let them know.

At the hospital, the nurse from the emergency room immediately came out to the car with a wheelchair, a towel, and an ice pack, while delivering a constant flow of reassuring words that they would have Mrs. Putnam put back together in short order.

"Oh, Mrs. Putnam, I'm so sorry about that fall. The same thing happened to me last year when I tripped over the dog. Those facial wounds always look worse than they really are. I have a towel and an ice pack right here for you. You just hold that in place so we can stop the bleeding. Here's a nice bed for you to lie down. I saw one of the surgeons in the hall a minute ago, and we'll get him to look at that wound. Everything is going to be all right."

The nurse took charge like a mother bear, arranging pillows, doing a quick neurological examination, calling in the doctor, scrubbing the area around the wound, and preparing all of the supplies for suturing. She hadn't bothered to ask the surgeon what he needed; she knew what he needed, and that was what he was going to get. She had already administered a tetanus shot and written the order in the chart, which only awaited the doctor's signature. If all of the doctors had disappeared, she could have expertly sutured the wound, too.

Service was personal at the Elliot Community Hospital; everybody knew everybody, and certainly, everybody knew Mrs. Putnam. The doctors all made house calls, even the surgeons, and they cared for the patients in the small hospital that had originally been a stately family residence on Main Street.

When it first opened, there were only eighteen beds, but eventually, the hospital needed more space, so the community got together and bought the large residence next door. Thornton Wilder mentions the Elliot Community Hospital in *Our Town,* his nostalgic play about a small, fictional New England community at the turn of the twentieth century, but the hospital in the play really existed in Keene, New Hampshire. It resembled tens of thousands of other "cottage hospitals" that served communities around the country in the first half of the twentieth century. In the basement, a group picture of the Cheshire County Medical Society, circa 1940, showed forty physicians who provided all of the medical care for the county's population of about forty-five thousand people.

In 1940, mothers and newborns made up most of the patients in the hospital, and they stayed two to three weeks after delivery to rest. The starched nurses' uniforms, the odor of disinfectants, and the signs prohibiting noise reassured the patients and visitors of a safe and sterile protective cocoon. Hospital-acquired infections from antibiotic-resistant bacteria never happened, because antibiotics did not yet exist. Doctors rarely performed surgery, and then mostly tonsillectomies, appendectomies, and some gynecological procedures. Patients who needed major abdominal surgery for gall bladder disease or cancer were referred to Boston where a small number of specialists had learned those newer operations. One room sufficed for the emergency room—it wasn't yet an emergency department—where general practitioners came in from their busy practices to set bones, apply casts, and sew up lacerations. One nurse managed the emergency room, and at night and on weekends, she served as the lone nurse in the hospital.

By 1970, the hospital had added some wings, but the emergency room still had only one room. New physicians and new ideas were coming. In the past, doctors had cared for even the sickest patients in their homes, because most effective hospital treatment didn't appear until the second half of the twentieth century. For example, less than 1 percent of drugs that we use today existed in 1940 when the photograph was taken. Included among the drugs that would not appear until the second half of the twentieth century were most drugs for heart disease and high blood pressure, diuretics, antibiotics, and cancer chemotherapy drugs. Doctors injected morphine to control pain in patients with heart attacks, but they had no other treatment, so patients lived or died in their own beds at home. Pneumonia killed as many people as it had during the nineteenth century. Physicians in 1940 had a more kindly bedside manner and were more likely to use encouraging words, because they had very little else to offer to their patients.

Since Marion Putnam's accident occurred in 1970, and not 1940, the doctors admitted her to the hospital for observation in case there might have been any bleeding inside her head. If they observed any change, they would immediately transfer her to Dartmouth Hitchcock Medical Center in Hanover for neurosurgery. The consequences of bleeding into the brain sometimes don't appear until several hours after an accident.

However, the next morning, Mrs. Putnam's status was deemed stable, and her doctor wrote an order that she could go home. What he hadn't realized is that her mental state was anything but stable. Two days before, she had been a proud, independent New Englander, but now she had lost all confidence. How would she manage simple chores, like making her own meals and dressing, when she was constantly in danger of falling? Because this was a small New England town, the hospital kept her for a few more days, and then a few more, hoping that she would again find the strength to resume her former life. She never did.

Her doctor consulted a psychiatrist and a social worker. She had no family support; her son was busy with his work and his own family in Boston, and her niece was busy raising three children. The only solution was to transfer Marion to a nursing home where she could receive help with the necessary "activities of daily living." She entered into a deep depression.

There was no garden that needed care, no chickens or goats to feed, and no children came to visit. She read a little, but no one in the nursing home wanted to talk about her books with her, and then the television set blared all day.

Marion Putnam died two years later of "old age."

Like old Mrs. Putnam, Elliot Community Hospital had become a relic of an earlier time, too, and had neither the space nor the modern equipment to keep up. The doors finally closed in 1972, the same year that Marion Putnam died, giving way to the brand new 150-bed Cheshire Hospital on the edge of town. The hospital staff would grow to 140 physicians because of an explosion of new medical specialties and subspecialties. Even so, the new hospital couldn't keep up with the rapidly evolving specialization of medical treatment. Heart surgery, neurosurgery, transplants, and many other advanced services had to be referred to Dartmouth or to Boston. Today, the hospital has a partnership with Dartmouth Hitchcock Medical Center to fill in the large variety of subspecialties.

The number of laboratory tests ordered reflected the huge changes in hospital practice. One analysis showed that the average number of tests ordered during a hospital stay rose from three in 1950, to six in 1960, to sixty by 1970. The complexity of treatment gave rise to new subspecialties that physicians in the 1940 photo could never have imagined. For example, some internal medicine specialists became cardiologists, and then some cardiologists specialized further in cardiac catheterization and coronary angioplasty, pacemaker management, cardiac electrophysiology, transplant management, pediatric cardiology, or preventive cardiology. A full complement of specialists became possible only in a large referral center, like Dartmouth Hitchcock.

Some internists stopped seeing outpatients and became hospitalists or intensivists concentrating only on inpatients, or sometimes on just the most critically ill patients in intensive care units. The ICU attracted bright young physicians.

"I love working in the ICU, because it is like a dynamic human physiology laboratory. We read a continuous flow of data, such as venous blood pressure from a catheter placed in the vena cava, and then adjust the dose of medicine that we infuse through the IV. We can then watch directly the resulting change in arterial blood pressure by reading from a different catheter placed in an artery in the wrist, and at the same time, we can look at improvements in the oxygen level in the patient's arterial blood. We have complete control of the patient's vital functions and can act instantly with any sign of deterioration."

Monitors now display composite graphs of real-time data, so that a physician or nurse can see at a glance any changes in the function of a patient's organs, and the information can now be relayed to portable handheld devices in case the intensivist leaves the bedside.

The quantity and variety of complicated equipment that specialists need to care for a single patient often completely surround a bed and blocks access to the patient. ICUs can dehumanize people. The cacophony from all the machines never stops, so the signs prohibiting noise found in early twentieth-century hospitals disappeared. Hospitals now resemble factories operating around the clock. The medical Industrial Revolution has arrived. Doctors no longer need to talk with patients. We have machines and monitors to tell us all that we need to know. Treatment outcomes have greatly improved, at least as measured by longevity and organ function.

The lives of Marion Putnam and the Elliot Community Hospital paralleled each other. Both were born late in the nineteenth century at the end of a rural culture where human relationships were close; family, neighbors, and friends helped each other and cared about each other. The Industrial Revolution, and later the information technology revolution, changed everything. In the twentieth century, families spread out around the country and around the world wherever their work or their desires took them. We all became restless—and impersonal. Marion Putnam and the Elliot Community Hospital were too old to adapt.

The Old Bicycle Racer

I couldn't tell his age. No visible fat showed on his five-feet-six-inch sinewy frame, and he reminded me of a weathered old jockey, or maybe a gnome under a bridge. I guessed his age at close to seventy years, and he looked at me sideways, correcting me.

"No, I had my ninetieth birthday last week."

To my amazement, he had never been to see a doctor and was here only because a health insurance company insisted. Perhaps they just wanted to reassure themselves that he was a real living person, because he had never submitted any claims. He had grown up in Italy, and when he immigrated to the United States only a few years before, he chose to live in San Jose to be close to a velodrome.

"Do you like to watch the bicycle races?"

"Yes, but I ride, too, and I coach the young riders. Back in Italy, age caught up with me as a competitor, and they have more than enough coaches. A lawyer in a cycling club here in San Jose helped me get a visa."

Many Americans past the age of sixty-five lack the agility and balance to ride a bicycle, but this ninety-year-old man was not only riding every day, he was riding on a banked track where crashes can be spectacular.

"Aren't you afraid of injuries?"

"Of course, but I've been doing this for many years, and I know how to stay out of trouble, and I don't compete in races anymore."

I knew a little about road racing from watching *le Tour de France* on television, and because pelotons of amateur racers on training rides come through my town of Portola Valley every day. Road races will cover one hundred miles or more in four or five hours, but racing on the track lasts only minutes and requires explosive bursts of energy and strength. Track bicycles are built for speed and weigh only about twelve pounds; they don't have any gears or breaks. Riding bicycles at a velodrome did not seem a suitable sport for a ninety-year-old.

I asked the patient if he had ever competed in road racing, and whether he had considered stepping down to bicycle touring, because with his small size, he looked as if he might have been a good climber. Touring doesn't require sudden acceleration like on a track.

"No, there are lots of good road racers in Italy, and I never had the opportunity. I've always specialized in track racing."

He had never suffered any serious illnesses and had never taken any medicine. His past injuries were only scrapes and bruises, except for a possible fracture of his forearm that must have knitted on its own. I asked about his diet.

"I don't like American food. I eat mostly pasta with tomato sauce, beans, vegetables, fruit, and some fish once in a while."

"How about alcohol and tobacco?"

"I used to drink wine once in a while in Italy, but it's too expensive for me here. I've never smoked. Nobody in my little town in Italy could ever afford that kind of luxury."

Here was a living example of the real Mediterranean diet: no red meat, butter, or anything wrapped in colored cellophane. If everyone followed his example, we physicians would have nothing to do.

I noted his resting pulse of 60 and his blood pressure of 110 over 60, typical of a twenty-year-old, unusually good for a fifty-year-old, but unheard of in a ninety-year-old man. His teeth were not perfectly aligned, but were completely free of dental caries, and upon examination his heart and lungs were normal. When I broached the subject of a rectal examination, his facial expression revealed part of the reason this was his first visit to a doctor in ninety years. He harbored a fear that doctors would find something bad. However, after explaining the importance of the exam, and why every sensible person should undergo this rude invasion, he acquiesced.

To my horror, a hard prostate nodule poked me in the finger. The chances of this being anything except cancer were slim. I had to recommend a consultation with a urologist, and to advise the patient to undergo some tests to uncover any evidence of spread outside of the prostate gland. The urologist was almost certainly going to advise a biopsy to confirm the diagnosis. I had opened Pandora's box.

A few days later, all the answers came back. Yes, the biopsy showed that it was cancer. No, there was no evidence of spread beyond the prostate gland.

The urologist and I talked about it. Published guidelines recommended offering surgery for healthy men under the age of seventy, but for men older than seventy years, or for younger men in poor health, the recommendation was either radiation therapy or "watchful waiting," which means no treatment at all. Long-term observations had shown that older men with prostate cancer rarely die of their prostate disease, but rather, they will more likely die first from something else, like cardiovascular disease. According to the textbook, this was a clear case where we should offer the patient either radiation or watchful waiting.

Most physicians would urge the latter, reasoning that the average life expectancy after age ninety is just a few years, and that the patient's cancer would probably remain dormant during that time. Autopsies performed on older men who died from diseases other than prostate cancer had shown that more than 90 percent of men at age ninety have cancer cells in the prostate gland, yet very few men past the age of ninety ever die of metastatic prostate cancer. On the other hand, surgery for prostate cancer entailed a risk; many things can go wrong during an operation, and the patient might suffer urinary incontinence as a complication.

None of the clinical studies on men with this disease gave me much comfort, however, because my ninety-year-old patient did not fit the average American mold. Life expectancy data didn't seem very relevant in his case. None of the ninety-year-old men in any of the clinical studies rode racing bicycles, and regarding the men in the autopsy studies, researchers usually found only microscopic cancer cells, and not an easily palpable, rock-hard nodule.

We had to talk about the risks and consequences of treatment. The urologist, the patient, and I all knew that some of the risks involved a vulnerable part of the anatomy critically important to bicycle racing. Anyone who has spent several hours on a bicycle seat knows that fatigue is not limited to just the legs. We call a pair of cycling shorts a chamois because of a strategically placed pad. Radiation, let alone surgery, would be disabling for a while, and possibly even end an activity that was an important part of his life and identity.

Of course the urologist and I could only advise the patient and provide him with information based on published data and our own experiences. The patient listened and weighed the potential risks and benefits. As soon as we finished, he immediately rendered his decision.

"I've been doing watchful waiting for ninety years, and I don't see any reason to change now. If the operation might prevent me from riding again, I don't want it."

Both the urologist and I reassured the patient that most experts would have concurred with his decision, and that we also agreed. The patient was unwilling to risk his present fulfilling years for an unknown situation and an uncertain future. It was perfectly reasonable.

I didn't anticipate seeing him again anytime soon; he had been quite happy to distance himself from anyone wearing a white coat. For months, I had the intention of dropping in at the velodrome on the chance of seeing him but always found a good reason to put it off.

About a year and a half later I saw him in the corridor of my medical office building. He had been having some persistent back pain that he attributed to his cycling and had dropped in at the emergency department. They had taken some X-rays and then called his urologist, who had just seen him. I called the urologist.

"It wasn't back strain from cycling. He has bone metastases to his spine from the prostate cancer. He's stoic, but I suspect that the pain is severe. He probably has metastases in his liver, too."

I felt sick. My intuition had told me that this ninety-year-old man was really thirty or forty years younger, physiologically, and that we should ignore observations based on large numbers of elderly men who did not fit the patient's profile. I philosophized that making a prognosis in medicine was like picking the winner in a cycling race. We know that the best rider is not always the winner, but that's the way to place the bet. Watchful waiting had seemed the best choice at the time. Given the same situation in the future with another healthy ninety-year-old man, I would probably come to the same conclusion that the risks of surgery outweighed the potential benefit, and that the best option was watchful waiting. We should always go with the head and not with heart—or should we?

In the end, the patient had made his own decision, but he certainly had to have sensed my leanings and those of the urologist. Helping a patient choose between two bad options is one of the hardest tasks that a doctor faces. The best rider doesn't always win.

The Serendipity Syndrome

He complained of "a little ol' backache—it ain't nothin' much."

His boss told him to come in to be checked, so he didn't have a choice; otherwise he would never have come. He had been breaking in mustangs and "got my back twisted up a bit." It happened from time to time, but aches and pains were just a normal part of his life. He had never been in to see a doctor except for one time about twenty years before.

"My back got broke, but it healed up pretty good."

He looked old to be a cowboy, and the chart confirmed his age at fifty-nine years, but his lean physique, dark leathered skin, bowed legs, and western drawl confirmed his occupation. The holes in his faded jeans and flannel shirt, and his dusty, weathered ten-gallon hat were authentic workman's clothes. Because of wrestling with horses and steers in the dust all day, shining his boots would have been a waste of time, so they resembled the color and texture of the fence posts in the corral where he yanked and shoved rebellious colts. His gnarled hands were twice the size of my own and were adapted to grabbing the reins, pulling on a rope, or tossing a bale of hay.

At the hospital, we see plenty of urban cowboys with pickup trucks, but information technology had transformed San Jose from an agricultural center to a part of Silicon Valley. The typical San Jose cowboy uses his pickup to commute to Cisco, or Intel, or SUN Microsystems where he works as an engineer, an accountant, or a marketing executive. My real wrangler represented a bygone era and looked nothing like the denizens of the computer industry or the romantic western heroes of Hollywood.

His friends called him “Sooner,” because he had been born in Oklahoma, but the chart named him Charles Stillwater Harvey, born 1920. As a teenager, he had come to California with his parents in the great migration during the Dust Bowl of the 1930s, an event that some Oklahomans today assert improved the IQ in both states. He had always worked as a wrangler and had never been to high school. Recently, he had been working on a ranch “a fair piece south of San Jose” in the hills that John Steinbeck had called “East of Eden;” the old cowboy would have fit perfectly as a character in one of Mr. Steinbeck’s novels.

On the ranch, Sooner helped care for a large stable of horses, a huge herd of steers, some cows, and a few “big ol’ bulls.” In the early spring, the herd could graze on the lower levels, and then as they depleted the grass, Sooner and some seasonal Mexican hired hands would drive the herd to higher levels just like a cattle drive in a movie about the old west. In the dry summer season, they would have to truck in feed for the animals that they confined in giant pens resembling old Chicago feedlots.

Many years before, Sooner had participated in rodeos and used to ride those “big ol’ bulls.”

“I was throwed a bunch back then when I was a young’un, but I take care now.”

“Breaking in colts doesn’t sound like taking care.”

“Heck, if you knowed how to do it, it ain’t nothin’. You just have to watch not to scare ’em. I ain’t been throwed for a long time.”

“What happened this time?”

“This colt was different. He had a mean look. I shoulda knowed.”

The patient had some obvious muscle spasm and stood tilted forward to guard against the pain. He couldn’t bend at all, but his neurological examination was normal.

“We’ll have to get some X-rays.”

The films did not show any fracture. What they did show was an ugly-looking spot on a lumbar vertebra, with an even uglier comment by the radiologist suggesting that the dense spot resembled metastases from prostate cancer.

I called the patient back in and told him that the X-rays suggested something wrong with his prostate gland, and that I would have to do a rectal examination. This was obviously going to be a first-time experience for him, and he eyed me with suspicion, but after a certain amount of coaxing, he acquiesced. To my horror, there was a one-centimeter firm nodule on his prostate gland, evidently the source of the metastases on the spine X-rays that the radiologist had reported. I would have to explain my concern to the patient and to refer him to a urologist for a biopsy to confirm the diagnosis. Meanwhile, I requested the usual blood tests that would help assess the magnitude of the extent of the spread of the cancer.

The patient bore all of this as a stoic and made an appointment to see me a few days after the biopsy to hear the results. Meanwhile, the laboratory tests returned showing an elevated serum calcium, typical of someone who might have widespread prostate cancer metastases eating away bone. As cancer displaces bone, it sometimes liberates large amounts of calcium into the bloodstream. I didn't look forward to explaining all of this to the patient.

The urologist called me with the pathology report from the biopsy.

"It's a benign prostate nodule."

"No cancer?"

"None, completely benign."

"But what about the X-rays and the elevated serum calcium?"

"That combination almost always means prostate cancer with metastases to bone—but not this time. He could have a small focus of cancer in another part of his prostate gland, but I couldn't feel anything else when I examined him. Can you do a bone biopsy of the spot on that vertebra?"

"I suppose so, but it would be a fairly major procedure. We might try looking around for evidence of other metastases that would be easier to biopsy."

"Has he ever had back X-rays in the past."

"He told me that he hadn't been to see a doctor for twenty years, so any X-rays that old have probably been destroyed. But I'll ask him. We can always try."

I told Sooner the good news and asked him if he had ever had back X-rays in the past.

"Yup, when my back got broke twenty years ago."

"Will you sign a release for us to send for them?"

"Sure."

He gave me the name of a tiny hospital in a small town in the San Joaquin Valley of California. I wasn't sure the hospital still existed, but it turned out that it did. Moreover, they still had the X-rays in their file and would send them to us. It was a miracle. My hospital sent out X-ray films more than two years old for storage, and recycled films more than ten years old to recover the silver that coated the films.

When the old films arrived, I took them to the radiologist for a comparison with the patient's recent films. That same ugly dark spot of exactly the same size existed twenty years before in exactly the same location on the same lumbar vertebra. Moreover, there was no evidence of an old fracture. Apparently, he had never had a broken back. The radiologist stared at the films.

"I guess that spot can't be metastases from prostate cancer. It must be something else, but I don't know what. I've never seen anything like it that wasn't cancer."

"That's great news for the patient, but he's going to think we're a bunch of quacks. I think wranglers aren't noted for having a lot of confidence in doctors. I still have to deal with the problem of an elevated serum calcium, but at least I won't have to go on a wild goose chase looking for metastases of a prostate cancer that doesn't exist."

The other blood tests suggested that the cause of the high serum calcium level was probably an excess production of parathyroid hormone, usually from a small benign nodule in the neck adjacent to the thyroid gland. Since the serum calcium elevation was only moderate, one possibility was to leave it alone and just watch. The danger of waiting would be the potential for the patient to form kidney stones or to leech calcium from bone causing osteoporosis, not a good disease for someone who makes his living as a cowboy.

I explained the dilemma to the patient telling him about the risks and benefits of treatment versus just watching. The only treatment was to remove the offending parathyroid nodule with a surgical operation on the neck. Sooner made his decision in a blink.

"I came in because of a little ol' backache, and now I'm healed up. I don't need no neck surgery. I'll let you know if I need any more doctorin'."

A year later, Sooner needed more "doctorin'." He had a kidney stone and was suffering a lot of pain. Through the magic of morphine and a little time, he passed the stone and "healed up." I asked him if he wanted to reconsider the neck surgery to remove the offending nodule in his parathyroid gland, but he adamantly refused.

"There ain't no more pain. I don't need no surgery."

"You may be vulnerable to more kidney stones."

"I'll take my chances."

Within six months, he passed another kidney stone, although with more discomfort this time. I asked if he wanted to reconsider the neck surgery. This time he did.

A few weeks later the patient had his neck exploration, and the surgeon removed a small benign parathyroid nodule. His serum calcium level and all the rest of his laboratory tests went back to normal. I told Sooner that he probably wouldn't have any more kidney stones.

I was wrong. A year later, Sooner had a third kidney stone, and then several more over the next few years. Kidney stones are fairly common, and in more than 90 percent of the cases, we never find a cause. Only in a minority of cases do we ever find the reason, such as a high serum calcium level from a parathyroid nodule. Sooner had both kidney stones and a parathyroid nodule, but they were not connected as cause and effect, just a very rare coincidence—serendipity.

Parathyroid nodules often cause kidney stones, but not always. When they occur at the same time, but are unrelated, we call it "the serendipity syndrome," a little trick that the gods of medicine play to keep doctors humble. Twice my patient exhibited combinations of symptoms and signs that pointed to a single definite diagnosis. Twice those combinations proved completely unrelated, a thousand-to-one long shot. A doctor could practice for a lifetime without ever seeing "the serendipity syndrome." With the old wrangler, I was stung twice.

Sooner took it all in good humor.

"That's all right, doc, I never figured that doctorin' was an exact science. But if I ever get my back twisted up again, I'm gonna hide out somewheres. I ain't comin' in."

I saw him again only a few more times over several years as the frequency of his kidney stones diminished. He never failed to warn me not to do any more of "them dang tests."

Dr. Gilbert's Patients Are Tired of Waiting

The patients were angry. Six of them remained, and three had been waiting for more than two hours. Only eleven were scheduled for Dr. Gilbert that morning, and now that it was almost noon, he was just starting on his fifth. The charge nurse in the urgent care center began her regular ritual of begging the other doctors to forego their lunch break in order to see the rest of the patients. The doctors would snap at her, because they would have a long day again with no time for a short break. It happened every time Dr. Gilbert was scheduled to work, and nobody was fixing the problem.

Ten years before, Dr. Jeffries, the director of the urgent care center, had encouraged Dr. Gilbert to join his staff at the hospital. Dr. Gilbert had built a successful family practice with a huge number of loyal patients, but the long hours and frequent calls at night exhausted him. He had blamed the constant demands of his practice for his divorce, but at forty-eight years of age, he still possessed plenty of vigor. The regular hours as a member of a group practice seemed to be a good solution that would allow him to remain busy as a clinician, and he would have time for more recreation and relaxation.

Dr. Gilbert's passion had been ice hockey, not just as a spectator, but as a player, too. He had been born and raised in Canada and liked living in San Jose because he could participate in an amateur ice hockey league and watch the Sharks play. His son also played hockey, and was thought to have had enough talent to become a professional player. Dr. Gilbert's new position at the hospital was going to allow him to put his life back together and to spend more time with his son. He would also have more time for reading; French language novels had been his special interest in the past.

He enjoyed the eight-hour day at the hospital where he saw twenty to twenty-five patients, only about three per hour. In his former practice, he had seen twice as many. The patients had the same problems: bronchitis, bladder infections, backaches, sprains, cuts, and gastroenteritis. Occasionally someone would come in with unstable chest pain, acute respiratory distress, or abdominal pain, and he would call for the internist on duty to come to admit the patient to the hospital. All in all, it was a fulfilling practice, and he felt he was making a contribution to the community.

The slower pace allowed Dr. Gilbert to gossip with the nurses and other physicians and to discuss interesting patients. A particularly close friendship blossomed with Dr. Jeffries who enjoyed Dr. Gilbert's company. Dr. Jeffries enjoyed telling a good joke, and Dr. Gilbert was always read to hear it. Both of them were experienced and efficient at taking care of common general medical problems, so they had plenty of time to kibitz between patients. Dr. Gilbert remained a valued colleague for nearly ten years.

The trouble first emerged during an inspection of the hospital by the Joint Committee on Accreditation of Hospitals (JCAH) when an auditor found one of Dr. Gilbert's charts to be illegible. Unfortunately, the charts were illegible to Dr. Gilbert, too, who was often unable to interpret what he himself had written. His handwriting had never been good, but since joining the staff at the hospital, it had deteriorated so much that even the charge nurse could no longer read it, and ordinarily, she could read anything doctor-written. The Quality Assurance Committee was going to require him to attend a course on handwriting that the hospital had organized at the insistence of the JCAH.

A year later, Dr. Gilbert began taking longer with his patients and requiring more time to complete his charts, still illegible. He started working through lunch and staying late in the evening in order to finish. Then he tried reducing his schedule to half-time and eliminating his turn working nights. Only one physician worked on the late shift, and Dr. Gilbert was no longer efficient or reliable enough to handle the load. Other physicians grumbled that Dr. Jeffries was showing favoritism to his old crony by excusing him from night duty. Finally, Dr. Gilbert started falling an hour or more behind on his patients, and he began missing important diagnoses. He sent home a patient with asthma who reappeared in the emergency department in distress only two hours later. Then he missed a diagnosis of acute appendicitis in a patient whose appendix later ruptured.

Dr. Jeffries couldn't bring himself to confront his friend, but the charge nurse wasn't going to allow the bad situation to continue. She skirted around Dr. Jeffries and the director of nursing and came directly to me in my capacity as the physician-in-chief. I called Dr. Gilbert to come to see me as soon as possible. Dr. Gilbert went first to Dr. Jeffries.

"The physician-in-chief wants to see me. That usually means bad news. Can someone finish seeing my patients?"

"Don't worry. He's a nice guy. I'll take care of your patients. You go ahead upstairs to see him."

Dr. Gilbert appeared in my office looking slightly disheveled; his speech and his movements were slow, and he seemed anxious and depressed.

"Are you going to fire me?"

"I just want to talk to you. The charge nurse tells me that you're unable to see most of your patients. She says it takes you half an hour to write a note in the chart, and even then she can't read it. What's wrong?"

"I don't know. I can't seem to concentrate."

"What have you done about it?"

"I set my alarm clock for five o'clock in the morning and drink a whole pot of coffee so I can get dressed and come to work on time, but the nurses still yell at me."

"Have you seen a doctor yourself?"

"No."

"Have you been drinking?"

"No, I don't drink."

"Are you taking any medicine?"

"No."

"Do you have a problem that is distracting you from your work?"

"No, I don't know what's wrong."

"I'm going to order a few metabolic tests and ask the chief of neurology, Dr. Gregory, to see you. I'll ask the chief of psychiatry, Dr. Joyce, to make an appointment for you, too. Meanwhile, I'm placing you on medical leave until we can get to the bottom of this."

Dr. Gilbert looked relieved. He wasn't going to be fired, at least not now, and maybe he did need to see a doctor. It hadn't occurred to him. A few days later, Dr. Gregory examined Dr. Gilbert and went over the laboratory tests and an MRI of the brain. Then he called me.

"I can't find anything wrong with Dr. Gilbert. He can do simple calculations accurately and has good recent recall. He certainly remembers his meeting with you. I find nothing focal in his physical examination or on his MRI, and all his laboratory results are normal. He has no evidence of a brain tumor, and I can't call him demented."

"What do you think about his capacity to practice medicine?"

"That's hard to say. He's a pretty intelligent fellow and could lose a large portion of his mental capacity before it became evident. Have you asked Dr. Joyce to see him?"

"Yes, she's probably seeing him tomorrow."

Dr. Joyce called the next day.

"I just saw Dr. Gilbert. He's a charming man. I know you were worried about his being depressed, but he seemed fine when I interviewed him. I don't see anything wrong psychiatrically. Have you asked a neurologist to see him?

"Yes, Dr. Gregory called me yesterday. He couldn't find anything either. Do you see any evidence of dementia?"

"No, but early dementia is very difficult to detect in an intelligent person like Dr. Gilbert. We could do some psychometric testing, but I'll predict that we'll find nothing."

"Thank you for seeing him. I'll call you back later."

I called Dr. Jeffries in the urgent care center to ask about the duration of Dr. Gilbert's problems. In retrospect, Dr. Jeffries had noticed gradual deterioration in Dr. Gilbert's work for several years. This was not just a recent problem.

"Why didn't you say anything before?"

"Dr. Gilbert has been such a good colleague that I didn't want to notice that something was wrong. What are you going to do?"

"I'm going to protect the patients. That's my first responsibility and yours too."

Dr. Gilbert came in to see me a few days later. The disheveled appearance had improved somewhat, and he was anxious to know what I had learned from the consultants.

"They can't find anything. Your examinations and your tests were normal, but something is clearly wrong, and according to Dr. Jeffries and the charge nurse, the problem has been growing for more than a year. Apparently, you don't have any specific stressful circumstance in your life, and Dr. Joyce doesn't think you're depressed."

"What are you going to do?"

"I can't let you go back into the same situation. I think that would be bad for your patients, bad for your colleagues, and bad for you, too. Your sick leave will soon run out, and the only alternative would be to accept long-term leave without pay. I'm going to request that the long-term disability board consider you disabled and grant you early retirement. You would receive half of your full salary, your full healthcare benefits, and some tax breaks. The board might balk at my early retirement request, because I don't have any solid medical evidence of a disability, except for your inability to practice normally as a doctor, but I can be very persuasive, and I think your disability may be permanent."

Dr. Gilbert was stunned, but maybe relieved, too. He knew that he couldn't handle the work and was expecting to be fired. The solution that I proposed might allow sorting himself out again. Dr. Gilbert said he thought the decision was reasonable. I wrote to the long-term disability board.

"Dr. Gilbert's performance as a physician has gradually deteriorated over a period of at least one year to the point where he no longer has the judgment to make clinical decisions. He has missed diagnoses leading to delayed treatment of acute illnesses, and he regularly falls behind in seeing his patients, staying late after his shift to complete his clinical notes, which our Quality Assurance Committee still finds to be unsatisfactory. Neurology and psychiatry consultants could not find any measurable mental deficiency, but they also warn that measurable evidence of early dementia in intelligent patients is often not possible. In my opinion, Dr. Gilbert does have early dementia and should be offered disability retirement."

I called Dr. Jeffries.

"I'm going to try to get approval for disability retirement because Dr. Gilbert can't do the work and is a danger to his patients. Neither Dr. Gregory nor Dr. Joyce could make a definite neurological or psychiatric diagnosis, but obviously something serious is wrong. I'd like you to keep in touch with Dr. Gilbert to look for any further deterioration in his mental status."

The board accepted my recommendation. After retirement, Dr. Gilbert did not recover, but instead, became more and more reclusive. He refused any help from his old friend Dr. Jeffries and would not return telephone calls. About a year and a half later, he died suddenly of a myocardial infarction. He was only fifty-nine years of age, and the heart attack was the first evidence of his having had heart disease.

Whether or not he had been suffering from Alzheimer's disease was never confirmed. Certainly, he had never considered himself to be sick. As Dr. Gilbert's son no longer lived in San Jose, nobody was regularly checking, and no one knew for sure whether or not Dr. Gilbert's mental status had deteriorated further.

The Quality Assurance Committee had inaugurated a "physicians' welfare service" to help physicians with health problems that could potentially interfere with their patient care. The objective was to solve problems before a physician's incapacitation harmed a patient. Physicians sympathetic to the health problems of their colleagues would participate by offering their services free of charge. Everything would remain confidential unless there was imminent danger to a patient. Neither Dr. Gilbert, nor Dr. Jeffries, nor any of their colleagues ever felt comfortable about contacting the service.

Nobody doubted that Dr. Gilbert suffered some crippling mental or neurological disorder placing his patients at risk, but detection of the cause of his disability eluded two highly competent specialists who were aware of Dr. Gilbert's deteriorating work performance. Physicians concerned about patients' welfare asked themselves some interesting questions.

"How should we intervene in situations where a person in a critical job affecting other people becomes incapacitated?"

"Should we require mandatory retirement beyond a certain age for physicians, airline pilots, or presidents?"

"Who was the real president of the United States during the last year of Woodrow Wilson's second term after he had suffered a series of strokes?"

"Do we know if Ronald Reagan was mentally competent toward the end of this second term?"

No one had answers, but all were certain that the problem would recur.

The Housekeeper

Margaret Swanson looked old as she struggled with her mop to clean a cubicle, preparing it for the next patient lying on a gurney just outside. Friday nights in the emergency department exhausted her with one accident or combative drug addict after another arriving in rapid succession until the end of her shift at 11:00 PM. Babies were crying, and at least one patient was always screaming in pain or delirious from alcohol or drug withdrawal. On the overhead loudspeakers, the page operator added to the din with a continuous demand for doctors, nurses, X-ray technicians, laboratory technicians, and orderlies to respond to an urgent need somewhere else.

When she first started working in the hospital thirty years before, the emergency department had consisted of only three or four treatment cubicles and a waiting area. Now it consumed half of the ground floor of the hospital with its own self-contained operating room and portable X-ray machine. New houses, apartment buildings, and shopping centers had mushroomed around the hospital displacing the orchards and small vegetable farms of a former quieter era. Stanford University had given birth to Silicon Valley, and now, new companies were spreading out in all directions: Hewlett Packard, Intel, Cisco, Oracle, Google, Yahoo, SUN Microsystems.

The nurses yelled at her to hurry to make room for more patients as the ambulances rolled in. So many patients were either bleeding or vomiting that the cleanup took longer. No one ever thanked her, or even noticed her except when a cubicle wasn't cleaned quickly enough. She was sure that nobody in the hospital knew her name, except for the manager of the housekeeping service, and he had been searching for an excuse to fire her ever since his arrival a few years before.

She used to work in the operating rooms on the day shift, but cleanup between cases was "dead time," and the hospital couldn't afford to pay operating crews to sit around and drink coffee while a housekeeper took too long to clean a room. Anesthesiologists would become impatient and put patients to sleep on a gurney outside the operating room to recapture the time while she finished. The nursing supervisor in the OR suite screamed at the housekeeping manager that long turnaround times of operating rooms were destroying her budget, and she demanded the replacement of that incompetent, slow housekeeper.

For Margaret Swanson, the capability of working eight hours had long passed, so she invented little tricks to help her complete her shift. The complaining did not seem to diminish if she worked faster, so she worked slower. Moreover, she didn't clean the cubicles as completely as she used to. She no longer bothered to wipe down the gurneys with a disinfectant and didn't change the water and detergent in her mop bucket between cubicles. She began stretching out her work breaks and would find a nook to lie down for a while.

She suffered mild, but constant pain in her back and knees and made an appointment with one of the doctors to obtain some medicine to help relieve it. The pills did relieve the pain, and they also numbed her a little so she could glide through the day. She began taking more, and then more. Her doctor never gave her enough to last more than a few days, so she made appointments with another doctor, and then another. By juggling her appointments and her prescription refills, she could amass enough pills to generate that numb feeling around the clock. The nurses in the emergency department began to notice that she seemed distracted and confused, and they wondered if she were no longer mentally competent. The nursing supervisor found out her name and reported the situation to the hospital administrator, who called in the housekeeping service manager.

"What's wrong with your housekeeper, Margaret Swanson? The nurses in the emergency department think she may no longer be mentally competent."

"I've wanted to fire her for a long time, but she's been employed here for almost thirty years, and she does her work, barely. I was certain that the union would never let us fire her."

"How old is she?"

"Sixty-two."

"What do her annual evaluations show?"

"They were always satisfactory in the past, but I've always given her a low rating."

"You gave her low ratings, but did you ever give her an unsatisfactory rating?"

"No."

"We can't suddenly fire a thirty-year employee who has never had an unsatisfactory rating. You're right, the union would scream—and they would win."

"What can we do?"

"First of all, we have a complaint from the nursing supervisor, so we can require her to be examined for mental competency. If she's truly mentally incompetent, she can retire early on long-term disability. She should undergo a general health examination, too. "

The hospital administrator called me to ask if I would see an employee for possible long-term disability. I asked if she had been injured on the job, and he responded that she had not, but that the nurses were complaining about her mental status. I agreed to see her and called the nursing supervisor in the emergency department.

"The hospital administrator has asked me to see Margaret Swanson, one of the housekeepers who work in your area. What can you tell me about her?"

"I think she's demented. She's always been slow, but now she takes a half hour to turn around a cubicle, and she does a sloppy job. She works evenings when we're the busiest, and she creates bottlenecks that interfere with patient care."

Mrs. Swanson came in to see me a few days later. She looked much older than her sixty-two years and carried about fifty pounds too much weight. She had high blood pressure, and her chart contained laboratory tests documenting type 2 diabetes mellitus. She appeared depressed sitting motionless with a vacant smile, slurred speech, and a flat affect.

"How are you today?"

"I have lots of pain in my back and my legs."

"Just when you work?"

"No, I have it all of the time."

"What do you do to relieve it?"

"My doctor gives me some pills, but he never gives me enough. Can you give me a refill? My back and knees hurt so much that I can't make it through the day without the medicine."

She showed me one of her empty bottles that had contained hydrocodone, an addicting narcotic that could readily cause drowsiness. The date was only a week prior and the quantity prescribed enough for two weeks.

"No, my job is only to be sure that you are able to work, and from the bottle, it looks like this should have been enough for another week."

"The bottle fell over in the sink while I was washing the dishes and I lost most of the pills."

"I want to ask you a few questions."

In spite of her slurred speech, she answered my mental status questions accurately. She knew the date, where she lived, the names of nurses and doctors in the hospital, and could recall recent major news events. I asked her if she thought she was competent enough to work.

"I don't have any choice. I have to work for three more years to be eligible for my retirement pension and healthcare benefits."

I asked her about her social situation. She had married many years ago, but the marriage ended in a divorce a few years later, and she had never remarried. She never had children, lived alone, and claimed that she had no friends. She had never completed high school and mostly watched television when she was not working.

Her physical examination and X-rays showed some early changes of osteoarthritis, but nothing unusual for a sixty-two-year-old person. I had no doubt that she had pain from her hard physical work, but could see nothing objective that would qualify as a disabling injury. She also had a number of risk factors for cardiovascular disease including her obesity, high blood pressure, and diabetes, but they would not have disqualified her from working. I thought that her most immediate problem was the addiction and excessive sedation from the prescribed pain medicine that accounted for her flat affect, slurred speech, and apparent mental incompetence noted by the emergency department nurse.

I thanked her for coming in and told her that I would be contacting the hospital administrator. She asked me what I had found and whether she was going to be fired. I summarized my findings and told her that the most significant problem affecting her employment was the sedation that her pain pills caused. She replied that she couldn't work without the pills. I told her that whatever the outcome, addiction to pain medicine could not be an acceptable solution.

When I confronted the other doctors who had prescribed so much pain medicine, they responded that they did not realize other doctors were prescribing narcotics too, and then they accused Mrs. Swanson of being dishonest and manipulative. They also admitted that the easiest way they could shorten her office visit was to give her the prescription that she was demanding. I didn't find their arguments to be either persuasive or professional.

I called the hospital administrator.

He asked, "Do you think she is disabled?"

I said that considering her age, weight, and joint pains, I thought she would never be able to satisfactorily complete three more years of hard work cleaning cubicles in the emergency department. She did have high blood pressure, diabetes, and some relatively minor abnormalities on her back and knee X-rays, but not enough to justify calling her disabled. Nevertheless, I was willing to declare her to be disabled, especially considering that physical labor was the only work for which she was qualified, and hoped that the disability evaluation board would accept my recommendation in spite of the minimal objective evidence.

The board did accept my recommendation, and the patient received enough disability payments to carry her over until she became eligible for her pension at age sixty-five. In addition, her full healthcare benefits would continue.

After retiring, Mrs. Swanson wanted to continue to see me and drove in her dilapidated old car for her appointments. She continued to live alone and had not made any new friends. In fact, she was convinced that acquaintances at a senior center had rebuffed her. She had no special interests and watched many hours of television. In spite of her diabetes and high blood pressure, she made her ow meals from high-salt, high-calorie, frozen or canned prepared dishes. She liked ice cream. Her several nieces, nephews, and cousins never visited her or invited her to their houses.

In spite of my warnings about drug addiction, she started again to see other doctors and appeared in several emergency departments demanding pain medicine. She would tell busy physicians a convincing story about how much pain she was suffering, and they would capitulate and give her a prescription. The drugs caused her to be confused, and she fell once on the pavement outside her apartment building. Her landlord became alarmed about her constant slurred speech and periodic confusion, and he threatened her family that he was going to evict her.

Mrs. Swanson's family lost no time in rushing to my office to demand that she be committed immediately to a nursing home. I assured them that nursing homes admit people, not commit them, and that nobody would or could do anything without the patient's consent. I suggested to them that I try one more time to work with Mrs. Swanson to solve the drug addiction problem. They made an appointment for her for the next morning.

When Mrs. Swanson came in, she had her slurred speech and vacant smile as before.

"How did you get here today?"

"I drove my car."

"Did you know that state law requires doctors to send a report to the Department of Motor Vehicles if they suspect that a person no longer has the ability to operate a motor vehicle safely?"

"Would you do that?"

"Yes. Taking sedating drugs and then driving causes you to be a danger not only to yourself, but to drivers and passengers in other motor vehicles that you might hit. Go sit in the hospital cafeteria or the main waiting room, and then come back to see me this afternoon at three o'clock."

When she came back later, her speech was better, but she was complaining about needing her pain medicine. I told her that the pills had been causing so much sedation that her family and her landlord were convinced that she had Alzheimer's disease.

"They wanted me to recommend taking away your driver's license and to commit you to a mental institution. They think you are no longer mentally competent and a danger to yourself. You don't have Alzheimer's disease or any other form of dementia, but those pills make you seem like you do."

Because she seemed more alert, I let her drive home. I called her niece, who confiscated Mrs. Swanson's pain medicine and was willing to check on her every few days. The family members were surprised at the sudden disappearance of her confusion and slurred speech, and the landlord no longer threatened to evict her. Mrs. Swanson came to see me every week for a while, relieved that her somnolence and confusion had cleared. She always kept her appointments and always wanted to talk to me; no one else ever listened to her. After a while, she would ask me for pain medicine knowing that I would refuse, but she would try anyway. I suggested Tylenol, but she wasn't interested because she was searching more for an escape with the pain pills rather than strictly pain relief.

Periodically, she would appear again with her slurred speech and vacant smile. I knew she had manipulated another doctor to obtain pain medicine, and we would go through our drug withdrawal routine, but these episodes recurred less and less. I sent a visiting nurse to see her every week, using the management of her diabetes and high blood pressure as an excuse. The nurse helped her connect with a neighbor in another apartment, possibly the first friend she had made in years. The friend's son gave her a cat that became the focus of her conversation with me on later visits.

Ultimately, Mrs. Swanson stopped coming to see me. The visiting nurse contacted the neighbor and learned that Mrs. Swanson's family had arranged her admission to a nursing home. At first, the neighbor tried visiting the nursing home, but Mrs. Swanson was always heavily sedated and unable to talk.

Longevity in the United States has increased to almost seventy-eight years, while the cohesion of family and community has fractured. Some people thrive in their later years, but many others suffer depression, dementia, or just loneliness. They often lack the capability of finding new interests and become marginalized socially. Those who lack education or good health run the greatest risk. We create institutions that support basic activities of daily living, like eating, dressing, and going to the bathroom, but they may do little for the spirit.

Mrs. Swanson's only social connections were through her work with a mop where she had been nameless and faceless. Small as the job was, her retirement accelerated her withdrawal into an isolated void.

Old Doc Peters

All of his patients liked him. He knew everything there was to know about how to relieve common everyday symptoms, because he had seen it all tens of thousands of times. Doc Peters was now seventy-five years old and had practiced medicine nearly every day of his life since his graduation from Tufts University School of Medicine in 1925. He had spent a year as an intern at the Maine Medical Center in Portland before beginning his practice as a country doctor.

Back then, doctors knew how to prevent the spread of disease with disinfectants, clean handling of food and water, quarantine, and vaccination against smallpox. Some new immunizations had just been introduced, including a new modern vaccine against diphtheria that replaced the horse serum that so often caused serum sickness. Alexander Fleming had not yet discovered penicillin, and even the earliest antibiotics would not be safe enough to use for another twenty years. Most treatment that we take for granted today did not yet exist, although two Canadian physicians had just introduced the use of insulin from animal extracts as a successful treatment to control the blood sugar in diabetics.

After Doc Peters had practiced nearly fifty years in Maine, his son who lived in California convinced him to give up shoveling snow and scraping the ice off his windshield and move out west. The pictures of palm trees and casual living attracted old Doc, but within a week, he became bored. He had always been busy and had never learned to sit around, so he thought about looking for something to do. Nearby was a new Kaiser hospital with a busy group practice of mostly young physicians. Old Doc didn't think they would be interested in him, but it wouldn't hurt to ask. It happened that the flu season had hit with a vengeance at that time, so they were happy to see him and asked if he would be interested in working part-time. He was.

It was a perfect marriage. Most minor illnesses are self-limited and have no effective treatment, and since Doc Peters had practiced during earlier years when he could offer his patients few treatment options, he had become expert at calming and reassuring patients. More importantly, he reliably recognized when patients had serious illnesses that required specialty treatment. Since many specialists surrounded him in the clinic where he worked, he would only have to walk a few steps to obtain a curbside consultation and possibly make a referral. He gave the younger physicians lessons in bedside manners, and they updated his knowledge about new advances in diagnosis and treatment.

The young physicians recognized old Doc's good sense, and they enjoyed hearing his stories about his practice in the wilds of the state of Maine. They asked him to join the group full-time, and he quickly accepted. Substituting palm trees for pine trees hadn't made much difference to him, and the clinic was much more to his liking as a place to enjoy his retirement.

Doc Peters had spent most of his years in practice in the tiny rural town of Freeport, Maine, about twelve miles northeast of Portland. Today, Freeport attracts thousands of tourists daily off the Maine turnpike to the headquarters of L.L.Bean. It boasts the largest post office in the state, needed to handle all of the mail-order business, but during the 1920s, it wasn't much more than a general store catering to wealthy vacationing sportsmen. They sold locally made clothing, like rubberized boots, flannel shirts, and jeans, and you could also buy expertly made fishing flies, snowshoes, or an authentic Old Town canoe made from wood and canvas. Even back in the 1920s, the population of Maine exploded in the summer with people escaping the sweltering northeastern cities, but in winter, the whole state seemed to be hibernating.

Only a few hundred people lived in and around Freeport after Labor Day, but September and October were the best months of the year. The weather was still warm and both the mosquitoes and the tourists were gone. Freeport didn't have either a hospital or a clinic, so Doc Peters used the living room of his house as a medical office. The Maine Medical Center in Portland was the nearest hospital, but the roads were bad, and it could take nearly an hour to get there—if the weather were good. Most of the time, he did house calls driving around rural Maine on the dirt roads in his model-A Ford just like in the Norman Rockwell paintings.

In medical school and during his internship, Doc Peters had learned skills that helped him practice in his isolated small town. He could set fractures, apply plaster casts, reduce dislocations, sew up lacerations, deliver babies, and do minor surgery. The mortality rate from appendicitis at the turn of the century had been very high, and appendectomies had become relatively safe during recent years, so he leaned to do the operation. Surgery in the abdominal cavity carried a significant risk, and the appendix is notorious for being difficult to find, but he never had a fatality. His kitchen served as an operating room.

His wife, who had died before he retired from his practice in Maine, had been trained as a nurse in Portland, and she could assist him during deliveries, help putting on casts, and administer ether-drop anesthesia using a gauze mask. She would answer the telephone, although most people around Freeport didn't yet have them, and she would calm patients during an emergency when Doc was off at some remote farm taking care of another emergency. In a pinch, she could handle most emergencies by herself pretty well, too.

Doc liked to tell the story of performing an appendectomy in the kitchen of a farmhouse at night when the electricity had gone out. At the turn of the century, electricity had come to the big cities, like Portland, but now even tiny Freeport could boast about having electric lights, although they weren't yet reliable, especially during a storm. The farm had some gas lanterns, but they didn't produce enough light, so he fashioned a ramp to the kitchen porch and ran the front wheels of his model-A up to the windows and turned on the lights.

The patient was a sixteen-year-old girl with a two-day history of abdominal pain and loss of appetite, and she had started to run a low-grade fever. Doc noted guarding and tenderness of her abdomen and the absence of any bowel sounds. If her appendix had not yet ruptured, it would very soon, and the outcome might have been tragic. Small rural towns could not afford ambulances, and Doc thought about taking the patient to Portland in a car, but the muddy roads during a storm created too high a risk.

His wife gave the ether to put the young woman to sleep, and then held a gas lantern to add more light to the incision area. By then, Doc had done many appendectomies, and he prayed that this one would go well, because trying to find an appendix using a gas lamp could be trouble. Luckily, it popped into view almost immediately. The appendix had not yet ruptured, but it was greatly swollen and would have burst soon. The farmer and his wife knew the stakes were high and were enormously relieved with the successful outcome. At that time, everyone had a family member or knew a neighbor who had died from acute appendicitis.

During the winter, a model-A Ford wasn't of much use around Freeport. Several feet of snow blanketed the landscape from late October to early April, so the roads weren't passable. The railroads used snowplows, but keeping rural roads clear of the deep snow in Maine was completely impractical. Besides, at that time automobile engines would freeze up in the extreme low temperatures in Maine. Even today, Maine natives place electric warming blankets on their car engines overnight to assure that they will start in the morning.

Doc Peters and the handful of other people in the town who owned automobiles would put their cars up on blocks and empty the crankcase for the winter. Most people still owned horses, so the options for getting around were either a one-horse open sleigh or snowshoes. Doc made house calls with his sleigh, a necessity that wasn't as romantic as it appeared on Christmas cards. On some days in January and February, the temperature never rose above zero degrees Fahrenheit, and at night, it could drop to thirty below.

The long winter took a toll on many people. April always teased everybody with one or two warm days, but it was cold and rainy much of the time, and the snow never completely melted until the middle of the month. In late April and early May, the snow converted to mud; all of the natives called it "mud season." Leaves on the maple trees don't appear until mid-May, so April still feels like winter. Doc called it mud season for a different reason. On a good day only two patients would cry during a visit in his front parlor, but on a bad day, five or six would break down. Today we call it seasonal affective disorder, or SAD, but Doc said it was just the long winter and the mud. There were always one or two suicides every year about that time.

If patients had pneumonia or a heart attack, Doc took care of them in their own homes in their own beds. For pneumonia, there wasn't any treatment except to wait out the fever; either it would break or it wouldn't. Sympathy and good nursing care had to suffice. For heart attacks, Doc could inject morphine for the pain and keep the patient quiet with old-fashioned sedatives like chloral hydrate. Everyone knew the odds, but Doc was good at supporting the patient and family through crises. Even so, pneumonia and heart attacks killed about one-third of their victims.

Most people had a great fear of strokes, but family support for stroke victims was much better in rural Maine than in our urban culture today. Even so, people feared becoming a bedridden burden to a family struggling to survive in the harsh conditions. During the Great Depression, most of the people in rural Maine were very poor and subsisted on what they could grow, preserve, or make for themselves. But they always provided loving care for the elderly who could no longer contribute.

Maine natives had a term for a mild transient stroke that would not cripple its victim. They called it a "pin shock" and would be tremendously relieved whenever Doc used that term.

"Oh, is that all? Pshaw, I was worried that it might be something serious."

Sometimes a migraine causes a pin shock, but in older people, a clot or spasm in a small artery causes a temporary, incomplete interruption of the blood supply to an area of the brain. We know now that a more permanent and more extensive stroke is likely to follow within a year. During the 1930s, no treatment was available to prevent the inevitable—effective treatment for high blood pressure didn't appear until after World War II—but people were optimistic, and they were realistic about life and death.

For the most part, people who lived in rural Maine at that time enjoyed good health and a longer life expectancy than their urban counterparts. Most couldn't afford cigarettes, so they didn't develop emphysema or lung cancer, and they suffered fewer heart attacks. In addition, they couldn't buy cheap, convenient, high-sugar, high-calorie food either, so they didn't become obese and develop diabetes. They engaged in hard physical work before the term "physical fitness" became popular. Consequently, many children knew at least one living great-grand parent.

Modern medical treatment would not begin in the United States until after World War II. Although the new treatments that physicians learned in the second half of the twentieth century saved millions of lives, life expectancy improved only about ten more years. The rapid economic development and growing affluence brought with it overeating, cheap and convenient access to tobacco, a sedentary lifestyle, and fast automobiles. We squandered most of the benefit from new treatments by adopting unhealthy health habits. Most of the Americans who accounted for the new longer longevity were ones whose health habits paralleled those of the rural Maine natives of the 1920s and 1930s.

Doc Peters supplied a bridge for the young Kaiser Permanente physicians to an earlier time when people were healthier in spite of the absence of modern medical treatment. His presence added a new perspective for the young doctors about prevention of disease. He enjoyed his new practice in California, which he found to be quite easy. He didn't any longer set fractures, deliver babies, or perform appendectomies in remote farmhouse kitchens at night, and he no longer owned a horse and sleigh. He didn't have to get up at night to see patients either. The younger physicians took care of the seriously ill patients, and old Doc helped the patients who just needed to talk and to hear some good common sense.

The World Series Was Postponed Today

"I got one! A ticket to the third game!"

The company had held a lottery for the employees, and my son won one of the four corporate season tickets to the third game of the World Series. It was a good seat, too. He had previously obtained one of the company's tickets to a game early in the season, and the seats were on the first-base side, ten rows back. Perfect!

This World Series was special. The Oakland Athletics and the San Francisco Giants were playing—the battle of the Bay. You could actually see the Oakland Coliseum across the bay from the top of the escalator leading to the second deck at Candlestick Park. The world champion would come from the San Francisco Bay area for sure this year. It was the East Bay against the West Bay. The freeways would empty and the bars would fill as practically everyone who didn't have a ticket would find a television set. Both Bay Area teams in the World Series might not happen more than once in a lifetime.

The telecast for the game at Candlestick Park came on at 5:00 PM as fans coming from work were still filing into the stadium while the players were warming up on the field. The Goodyear blimp overhead gave a panoramic view of the stadium, the bay, and the city. Suddenly, the image began to break up and announcer Al Michaels started to shout.

"I'll tell you what—we're having an earth …"

The screen went blank for a few seconds before the network "rain delay" graphic appeared. Everyone in the Bay Area knew exactly what had happened and would remember exactly where they were and exactly what they were doing at that moment.

"I thought I had a flat tire. I could barely control the car. Looking ahead, I could see the street moving like a wave in the ocean."

"The whole building was swaying—maybe thirty feet from side to side. I was on the twenty-sixth floor at the Embarcadero Center, and I thought surely the building was going down."

"It was the noise! I never knew that an earthquake would be so loud. I was on the first floor, and I thought the whole hospital would collapse on top of me. There was dust everywhere."

"I only felt a little movement, maybe slightly more than the usual earthquake. Some water splashed out of the toilet and a few books fell from a bookcase, but that's about all. Up where I live in the hills, the ground is pretty stable, so we don't get much movement the way they do down low. The ground next to the bay is like Jell-O during an earthquake."

Forever after, everyone in the San Francisco Bay Area called it the World Series Quake, the first earthquake ever telecast live on national television. It happened at 5:04 PM on October 17, 1989, and it lasted fifteen seconds and measured 7.1 on the Richter scale, killing sixty-seven people. The epicenter of the quake was in an unpopulated area in the Santa Cruz Mountains near Loma Prieta peak, sixty miles south of San Francisco, but the worst damage occurred in the landfill close to the two ends of the San Francisco–Oakland Bay Bridge.

Forty-two fatalities occurred from the collapse of the double-deck freeway, called the Cypress structure, near the toll plaza in Oakland. Miraculously, some drivers and passengers on the crushed lower deck survived and were pulled from the wreckage, including some found alive days after the earthquake. The shock moved the Oakland side of the bridge seven inches to the east, and one section of the upper deck collapsed onto the lanes below. Luckily, traffic on the bridge was light because of the World Series, so only one person was killed. Some of the worst damage in San Francisco happened in the Marina District, which was built on top of rubble bulldozed into the bay after the 1906 earthquake. Fires broke out, just as in 1906, and television cameras recorded a San Francisco fireboat pumping water from the bay into the fire.

Fifteen miles from the epicenter, doctors and nurses at the Kaiser Hospital in San Jose felt the shock and began looking around to see if any patients were injured. None were, but everybody was anxious because the quake shook the building more than any prior earthquake since the hospital had opened in 1975. Many doctors and nurses were just finishing with their last patients of the day in the medical offices next door, so large numbers of them converged on the emergency department to offer assistance. The few patients remaining to be seen from before the earthquake never imagined they would receive such prompt attention by so many physicians.

One of the physicians who happened to be on duty in the emergency department was the chairman of the hospital's disaster planning committee, Dr. Patricia Black. She had organized a successful drill only the week before to practice with the communication equipment, organize the system of triage, assign responsibilities for specific tasks, and measure response time of critical support services. She immediately declared a state of emergency and initiated the hospital's disaster plan by contacting key hospital departments including radiology, operating rooms, intensive care units, the blood bank, and hospital administration. Electricity would not be a problem because the power was still on in San Jose, and the hospital had an electricity generator that would automatically turn on in case of a power outage. She broadcast a message on the hospital's loudspeaker paging system.

"This is an emergency! We have just experienced an earthquake of major magnitude and are anticipating large numbers of trauma victims. All surgeons with triage assignments should report to the emergency department immediately. All other surgeons, please report directly to the operating rooms. All internists and pediatricians should report to the intensive care units, hospital inpatient units, or urgent care center according to the disaster plan. Area supervisors should use walkie-talkies to contact the command center in the emergency department, because large numbers of incoming calls may jam the telephones."

The walkie-talkies were short-range radios that would help assure coordination of patient flow and instructions to doctors, nurses, technologists, orderlies, and support staff to go where they were most needed. Problems with the phone service would not affect the walkie-talkies. She also made shortwave radio contact with the county disaster response center and local ambulance emergency services to learn about the volume of incoming ambulances and estimates of numbers of casualties in various locations around the county. They did not yet have any information. She then organized two triage teams of surgeons and nurses in the parking lot outside the emergency department ready to receive ambulances as they began backing in. One of the assistant administrators stood ready to direct ambulances toward an available triage team.

Meanwhile, the hospital administrator and manager of the hospital engineering department were making an inspection of the hospital. A quick tour showed no evidence of major damage, but the engineer expressed fears about the elevators and raised concerns about their safety until he could do a more thorough examination. He recommended setting up temporary beds in the corridors outside of the emergency department and operating rooms, which were across from each other on the same floor.

The administrator called Dr. Black using a walkie-talkie.

"We can't use the elevators until the engineers do a complete check, which might take several hours. Housekeeping is setting up beds in the corridors outside the emergency department. I'll call the county to let them know our status. What have you heard so far from the ambulance services?"

"They don't have much information yet, but so far, no ambulances are en route to us. We've cleared out most of the patients who were here before, so we're ready to receive earthquake victims. I'll let you know as soon as I hear anything further from the paramedics."

The administrator checked a television monitor showing a local television channel that was functioning normally and broadcasting updates about damage from the earthquake. The announcer said that so far, San Jose had experienced some damage, but nothing major on the order of the disaster suffered in San Francisco and Oakland. The administrator called the county disaster control center.

"This is Mr. Johns at Kaiser Hospital in San Jose. We have no apparent major damage, but we're doing a careful inspection of our elevators, which might take several hours. Meanwhile we'll have temporary beds set up on the ground floor. Our emergency department, operating rooms, and radiology services are all working, so we're open to receive emergencies. What's the status of other hospitals in the county?"

"We've only heard from two other hospitals so far, and they have the same concern as you about their elevators, but both of them have a green light for ambulances. Keep us posted about your numbers of victims coming in and your capacity."

By six o'clock, the television channel was showing a few pictures of damage from around San Jose, but mostly they showed images of the Bay Bridge, the collapsed Cypress structure in Oakland, and fires in the Marina in San Francisco. The scene in the Marina resembled the chaos of the 1906 earthquake with buildings collapsed, fires out of control, and anguished victims. In San Jose, the earthquake completely collapsed homes in one neighborhood, but there were no deaths. Information was not available about the number of injuries. Televised views of the freeways and streets showed almost no traffic. Usually at six o'clock, that channel was showing helicopter views of the location of bottlenecks and motor vehicle accidents and was advising commuters about alternate routes. The empty streets were eerie.

Dr. Black called Mr. Johns.

"We're now an hour since the earthquake, and we've received no ambulances. Does the county center know we have a green light?"

"Yes, I told them. When I called, they had information from only two other hospitals, Good Samaritan and Santa Clara County. Both of them were on green to receive patients, but they're checking out their elevators just like us. I'll try to call them directly to find out what they know."

Good Samaritan had some damage, but they were fully operational except for the elevators, and they expected that they would be able to use them shortly. Only one ambulance had come in, but it was a medical emergency that had nothing to do with the earthquake. The county hospital also reported light activity in their emergency department.

By seven o'clock, Dr. Black had released one of the triage teams and had brought the other back into the emergency department. Inside, it was quieter than she had ever seen. No patients were waiting, and the cubicles were all empty. The operating rooms were empty too. She watched a television monitor for about fifteen minutes. The San Jose local channel showed scenes in San Francisco and Oakland, but not one word about the situation in San Jose. She called Mr. Johns again.

"Nothing is happening here except for a couple of patients wandering in for relatively minor injuries. Do you have any new information?"

"All the other hospitals in the county are reporting the same thing. A few patients with cuts and bruises have come in, but nobody has received any serious injuries. We haven't heard of any requests from emergency departments in San Francisco or Oakland for our help. All the hospitals seem to be operational and able to handle any emergencies."

Dr. Black notified all the physicians. The television monitor remained silent about any street closures from earthquake damage, so some of the doctors and nurses who lived near the hospital decided to try to go home. Others began looking for an empty bed in the hospital to spend the night.

By eleven o'clock, one of the elevators was fully operational. A few more patients wandered into the emergency room, but none with serious injuries, and the urgent care center next door was almost empty. By the next morning, the total count of patients seen between 6:00 PM and 6:00 AM was only thirty-two, and most of them had nothing to do with the earthquake. The count on a normal night would have been about 150 patients. The Kaiser hospital had seen a record low number of emergency patients for the night.

Hospitals all around the San Francisco Bay reported a lower-than-normal number of emergency patients. The earthquake injured 3,757 persons, but most of the injuries were minor. At that time, seventy hospitals existed in the Bay Area, so the average number of victims seen per hospital was only about fifty-five. The large San Francisco and East Bay hospitals received the lion's share, but even they reported lower-than-expected numbers of emergency patients. Enough other people must have stayed home to more than offset the increase due to the earthquake victims.

Why did people stay home? Analysts postulated many reasons. Television channels showed pictures of road blockages, the worst of which were the collapsed Cypress structure in Oakland and the upper deck of the Bay Bridge. Many people may have worried about being able to get through to the hospital. Most may have assumed that crowds of victims had overwhelmed emergency departments causing very long waits during the night. Since the roads were nearly empty, fewer motor vehicle accidents occurred, easing the pressure on emergency departments. The drama of the disaster mesmerized many people who didn't budge from their television set all evening. Everyone waited to see how the aftermath would affect their daily lives.

What would have happened if the earthquake had been worse? No one really knew the extent of the damage until the next day. Suppose there had been ten times as many victims, or worse. Suppose the earthquake had destroyed several hospitals and rendered many others minimally functional. The Kaiser hospital disaster plan could have handled large numbers of victims, but unforeseen bottlenecks would have occurred. The Loma Prieta earthquake revealed the elevators to be a weak link that could have sharply reduced the hospital's capacity to function. For several months, the doctors and nurses talked about what they might do in the case of a really big one. No one felt very confident.

Fewer fans watched the World Series of 1989 on television than at any time in recent years. The city of San Francisco had built Candlestick Park on a landfill, and the earthquake shook it badly. Engineers would not certify the upper deck safe enough to hold spectators, but the Oakland Coliseum across the bay had incurred only minimal damage, so the teams played the remaining games in Oakland beginning two days after the earthquake. Although most residents of the Bay Area remember that the Giants and Athletics played in the series, few can recall who won. It was Oakland, four games to none.

"Humanity has but three great enemies: fever, famine, and war; of these by far the greatest, by far the most terrible, is fever."

Influenza

I'm not sure anymore whether it really happened or was just a nightmare, but I remember that the location was Davis, California, back in the year 2010. It seemed out of place because the people who live there boasted about having the most environmentally conscious community in the world. They even built the famous Davis Toad Tunnel at a cost of fourteen thousand dollars for the overpass that crosses Interstate 80.

The new overpass displaced a dirt lot where toads had hopped from one side to the other, and animal lovers worried that cars on the overpass would kill the toads as they attempted to cross the road. To save the toads, the town built a tunnel twenty-one inches wide by eighteen inches high to give them safe access. Unfortunately, the toads refused to use it, so they added lights in the tunnel to attract them. Many toads died from the heat. Then birds discovered the exit hole on the other side and began attacking the toads as they emerged. That was front page news in the *Davis Enterprise.*

Davis lies between San Francisco and Sacramento, although much closer to Sacramento from which it is separated by the flood plain of the Sacramento River. During the summer dry season, the river slows and measures only about fifty or sixty yards across, but the heavy rainfall in winter brings a fast current that overflows the banks, flooding fields and spreading a mile or more on either side of the river. The silt that deposits in the Sacramento River Delta makes the soil fertile and creates one of the most productive rice-growing regions in the world.

In the past, after rice farmers had harvested their crop, they burned the remaining straw blotting out the sun with a black acrid smoke. Citizens in Davis complained and worked to pass an ordinance against the burning, so the farmers began flooding their fields and allowing the straw to rot in place. The ecological change attracted migratory ducks and geese that found the flooded rice fields a bountiful feeding ground.

The town enjoys perfect climate in spring and autumn, but winters bring cool, raw, rainy, foggy, barren, joyless days. The leaves and flowers have disappeared, and small shallow lakes flood the orchards, vineyards, and tomato fields surrounding the town. Yolo County produces more tomatoes, and more pizza sauce, than any other county in the United States. Scientists had even developed a special Yolo County hybrid tomato that resists bruising, so that big mechanical tomato-eating monsters could gorge themselves on acres at a time.

Summers are intolerable. The population dwindles, as anybody who can, leaves town. Early inhabitants planted thousands of sycamore and oak trees that now form a high canopy over the entire town, like a giant parasol, but nothing can adequately protect against the relentless baking sun and cloudless skies of summer. Temperatures soar to over 110 degrees Fahrenheit daily for a month at a time, and the residents have no option but to survive indoors in those days of fire. A fine grayish dust sprinkles every surface, like in a desert. In fact, the great central valley of California had been a desert in the Gold Rush days prior to the introduction of irrigation from reservoirs created behind the great dams in the foothills of the Sierra Nevada Mountains.

Almost none of the adults living in Davis were born there, and very few of them die in Davis, so the undertaking business isn't very active. Nearly half of the population of 65,947 is matriculated at the University of California at Davis, opened in 1908 as the University of California's University Farm. Most of the rest of the people either are employees of the university or perform services that support those who study, or teach, or do research there. Consequently, at least half of the population turns over every four years and thinks of home as somewhere else. Although Davis is a very friendly town, most of the people exist within their own private worlds of intellectual pursuits, or work to support someone who is absorbed in intellectual pursuits, and so social relationships are temporary. Most people are preparing for a future elsewhere, not living for the present. During vacation breaks, Davis empties, and those who remain may feel isolated and lonely—and sometimes relieved.

From April to October, the townspeople greet each other every Wednesday and Saturday at the famous Davis farmers' market and picnic in the park. They talk and listen to the music and buy their dinner from stands that sell homemade culinary specialties that recall a more agrarian time. During a two-week period, high school and junior high students perform plays as part of a program called Shakespeare in the Park.

But the big event happens at the end of April. Picnic Day! Fifty thousand people attend to watch the big parade of fire trucks, antique farm machinery, and environmentally friendly vehicles designed by future engineers. Children, horses, dogs, university clubs, and civic groups all march advertising their activities. And at the end of the parade, the 150-member UC Davis California Aggie Marching Band struts in their straw hats, white shirts, and blue jeans, blasting out popular rock music of the day. Then everyone disperses to attend some of the 150 free events including the Doxie Derby for Dachshunds, the sheep dog trials, the chemistry magic show, and especially, they want to see the fistulated cow. Veterinarians had fitted her with a plastic portal into her side to observe the digestion processes. Students named her "Hole-y Cow."

Davis brags of the greatest number of bicycles per capita in the nation, and cyclists can receive a traffic ticket for careless riding. Everyone rides to the right and follows strict rules in the roundabouts at the intersections of the bicycle paths. Cal Aggie Cycling enters teams in road racing, mountain bike competition, and track racing on velodromes. They won the national road racing competition in 1994, 2001, and 2006.

Town and gown relations are good with university students participating in many civic activities, such as the Davis Community Theater. The university invites townspeople to participate in certain courses of study, and also to attend the many cultural and athletic events on the campus. Everyone reads the *Davis Enterprise* to keep appraised of local events. Its editor quips that the newspaper is so small that rubber bands keep falling off, interfering with efficient home delivery.

Sometimes students run for election to the town council—and win, although some townspeople don't necessarily view that as a positive.

Such was the normal life in Davis, so that the inhabitants had little reason to anticipate the incident that took place that winter, or as everyone subsequently realized, were they able to appreciate the premonitory signs of the grave events that were about to descend upon them. An account of the first day needs some detailed explanation.

While he was peering out of his office window on the morning of December 14, Dr. Everett Spencer, professor of veterinary pathology, noted that one of the feral cats that prowled around his veterinary science building had died. A number of stray cats lived by hunting rodents and birds around the pond on the dammed-up part of Putah Creek. The arboretum along the creek exhibited a riparian ecology with an extraordinary diversity of plants that sheltered small animals. Students and visitors using the picnic grounds across the creek tossed the remnants of their food to the ducks that competed for the scraps.

An hour later while he was walking to a meeting, it struck him as odd that the cat had not crawled off into the brush to die, but rather, was just lying out in the open. He wondered if the cat had found some rat poison, or maybe someone didn't like the idea of feral cats killing small birds in the arboretum and intentionally left poisoned food for the cat. Worse, suppose the cat had died of an infectious disease, like rabies for instance? He didn't like that idea.

Then he was distracted in the lab until cycling home for lunch. The neighbor's four-year-old daughter rang the doorbell and was standing there with a dead cat in her arms.

"Dr. Spencer, can you fix my cat?"

"He looks very sick. How about if I take him for a while?"

"OK."

"Did the cat bite you, Suzie?"

"No."

Dr. Spencer grabbed a plastic trash bag and held it up as Suzie dropped in the cat, and then he called the child's mother.

"Suzie just came over with a dead cat. Have you had the cat for a while?"

"We don't have a cat."

"Do you know where she could have found this cat?"

"No."

"Do you know if the cat was alive when she found it?"

"No."

"I asked Suzie if the cat had bitten her, and she said no, but we can't know that for sure. I'm taking the cat into my laboratory for an autopsy. Perhaps you should call your pediatrician. You can let him know that I'll have the preliminary results of the autopsy in a few hours."

Dr. Spencer didn't use the word rabies, and now he hoped that both cats had fallen victims of some cat hater. He might know about the possibility of poison from the autopsy, and the thought gave him some solace. Then he thought about retrieving the first cat near his office window, but apparently, the groundskeepers had already picked it up. Finding that dead cat wouldn't be easy, and then maybe he was being too much of an alarmist.

The autopsy lab in the veterinarian sciences building was larger and more modern than the one at the medical school. He went to work immediately collecting stomach contents, specimens for cultures, and tissue samples for making slides. He opened the cranium for an examination and to make slides of the brain. Nowhere did he find any evidence of bleeding, so the rat poison idea was eliminated. What he did find surprised him: the cat had apparently died of pneumonia. He would still examine slides of the brain, but rabies was now very unlikely, and in fact, the death of the two cats at about the same time was probably just a coincidence. He began to accept the idea that he was just being overly cautious because of his neighbor's daughter, and began to concentrate on his research.

Late that evening as he was pedaling home, he passed rows of trash cans out on the curb waiting for the garbage company pickup early the next morning. On top of one of them was a dead cat. He resisted a strong urge to stop and pick it up and continued pedaling, but when he got home he thought again of little Suzie next door. He explained it to his wife.

"I've seen three dead cats today, and that's an odd coincidence. Little Suzie Chandler next door brought one in her arms to me, and I did an autopsy. The cat died of pneumonia. I passed the third dead cat in a trash can on my way home, and ordinarily I wouldn't worry about it, but in thinking about that child next door, I think I'd better go back and pick up the third cat."

Dr. Spencer grabbed another plastic trash bag and pedaled back to the trash can, put on surgical gloves to pick up the cat, and placed it in a refrigerator in the autopsy lab. He planned to have one of the veterinary medicine students do the autopsy the next day. Then he went back home for dinner.

The next morning, his voice mail had three recorded messages: Suzie's pediatrician, Suzie's father, and a local veterinarian who had two dead cats that he thought might have died of pneumonia. The vet wondered if Dr. Spencer had heard of any other cats dying of pneumonia. Dr. Spencer returned all of their calls and told them what he could. Then he went to the autopsy room where veterinary medical student, Michael Becker, was performing the autopsy. It was pneumonia again.

Dr. Spencer called one his colleagues, Dr. Spitzer, a virologist.

"Hi Spitz, I've got specimens from two cats that died of pneumonia, and I had a call from a local veterinarian who has seen two others. My bacteriological cultures from yesterday don't show anything so far. Can you do some viral tissue cultures for me?"

"Sure, no problem, Everett. Do you think that you have a feline epidemic?"

"Four cats dead from pneumonia at the same time is a bit unusual, and early yesterday, I saw a dead feral cat but didn't pick it up. So we may have as many as five cases in the same day. Pneumonia is common in cats, and ordinarily, I'd just wait and see. This might be just a coincidence, but a little girl was carrying one of the dead cats, and I think we ought to do what we can to find out why that cat died."

"We can also do electron microscopy if you like. That way we can tell you more quickly whether or not the cat died of a viral disease, but we may not be able to identify the specific virus."

"Sure, go ahead. Viral pneumonia is the most likely diagnosis in the cats, but it wouldn't hurt to confirm it."

Michael Becker, overheard the call.

"Do you think this will turn into something big?"

"I don't know, Mike, we need some more time and maybe some more cats to see what's going on. Why don't you call all of the local veterinarians on our list to see what you can learn?"

It was starting to rain, but Dr. Spencer wanted to think, so he put on his slicker and walked down the path that led to the pond by the dam in Putah Creek. On the other side, two of the feral cats had nabbed a duckling and were tearing it apart while fighting with each other. It wouldn't matter much, because Putah Creek was full of well-fed ducks even in the winter. Wild ducks usually flew farther south, but these ducks were practically domesticated as a result of all of the scraps of food from visitors to the arboretum. There was nothing more to do about this cat pneumonia situation except to wait for the culture results and to see if any more cats were dying. He walked back.

Dr. Spencer found Mike and asked what he had learned from the veterinarians.

"Three of them have had cases of cats dying, but none of them suspected any epidemic, so they cremated all but one of the cats. The vet hadn't had time to cremate that last cat, so he's bringing it in. All the vets asked that we keep them informed."

Mike Becker was a good student, compulsive and attentive to details. He commuted every day from Sacramento where he lived with his wife and infant son in a small apartment, because Sacramento was less expensive than Davis. Graduate students don't have a salary, so supporting his young family on borrowed money worried him. To make matters worse, Mike and his wife were both exhausted all the time, because the baby awoke and cried every few hours and wouldn't sleep without nursing.

Mike's wife took insulin for diabetes and was sick at times, so he worried constantly and was torn between his responsibilities at the vet school and at home. She was having more insulin reactions that always caught her by surprise. Sometimes Mike would get her to drink some orange juice in time, but at other times she quickly became incoherent and combative, refusing to swallow. He would then have to inject her with the glucagon that they kept in the refrigerator to raise her blood sugar level back up to normal. She would have complete amnesia for each of these frightening incidents. They didn't know what would happen if she had a reaction when Mike wasn't there. Neither of them had any family living near Sacramento.

On the morning on the third day, Dr. Spitzer called Dr. Spencer to tell him that a virus was present in the lung tissue on electron microscopy, possibly influenza, but that he couldn't be more specific. Soon after, Suzie Chandler's pediatrician called again.

"Mrs. Chandler brought Suzie in to see me this morning because Suzie awoke early with a fever, muscle aches, and a cough. It looks like influenza. Suzie had received a flu vaccine in October, but the virus can mutate between the date of production of the vaccine and the onset of the winter flu season. I ordered a PCR test for influenza A, and it was positive, but I don't know what this might have to do with a dead cat."

Dr. Spencer responded, "At least two of the cats died of what looks like viral pneumonia, possibly influenza on electron microscopy, but domestic cats are not usually susceptible to human influenza A infection. However, virologists found some cases of avian influenza A in cats in Asia and also in Germany a few years ago. They found it in a few other animals too, including pigs and a dog. It's highly contagious among birds. You remember the cases in Southeast Asia where a number of humans handling domestic ducks and chickens acquired avian flu? The mortality rate was high, too, around 60 percent, I think, but the outbreaks ended abruptly for reasons that were never clear. They also found a few cases where they suspected human-to-human transmission. The authorities destroyed millions of chickens and ducks. But I've never heard of a case of avian flu transmitted from a cat to a human. If you send us a specimen from Suzie, Dr. Spitzer here is doing viral tissue cultures on the two dead cats that we have, and we can add her specimen to see if the subtype matches. If it does, we may be seeing the first report of cat-to-human transmission of avian flu. I don't like that very much."

Tissue cultures can grow out a wide range of viruses and will identify the specific type and subtype. They are vital for identifying the specific influenza virus, such as Influenza A subtype H5N1, which caused the outbreaks in Asia and Germany. The drawbacks are that tissue cultures take more than a week, and most medical center laboratories don't have the capability to perform the test. Luckily, the UC Davis School of Veterinary Medicine school did have a virology lab. They would be able to document whether Suzie and her dead cat had the identical virus.

The pediatrician had made a diagnosis of influenza A with a test called a PCR, which stands for polymerase chain reaction. The test stimulates accelerated replication of viral DNA strands in a specimen to increase the quantity of DNA to an amount sufficient to allow rapid identification of the virus. The results can be available in only a few minutes, and the test accurately determines whether or not a specific virus or bacteria is present—if the requester knows which specific disease to look for, like influenza A. The pediatrician was anticipating the beginning of the annual winter flu season, and since Suzie had symptoms typical of influenza, he guessed that she had influenza A. He was right. However, typical human influenza A viruses are usually different from the ones found in animals.

Dr. Spencer and the pediatrician were still worried, because a number of cats were dead, and that meant if one of them had transmitted avian influenza to Suzie Chandler, they might be seeing the beginning of an outbreak more deadly than in the recent annual flu seasons with typical human influenza A viruses. Dr. Spencer and the pediatrician could be witnessing the beginning of a dangerous epidemic of avian influenza with a potentially high mortality rate. They also knew that the deaths reported from recent outbreaks in Asia were mostly in children and young adults, just as in 1918 and 1919. They would have to wait for the tissue cultures to know if the virus from the cats matched the subtype that they would find in Suzie's specimen. Dr. Spencer continued his phone conversation with the pediatrician.

"Are you seeing many patients now with flu-like symptoms? And do you know if other doctors have noticed any increase?"

"We always see a lot of upper respiratory illness this time of the year, but it's been relatively light so far—nothing that would suggest the start of the flu season yet. Sometimes it doesn't begin until late winter. If you'd like, I'll call around to find out if anyone else has noticed an increase."

Dr. Spencer remembered the dead feral cat near the arboretum and decided to take another walk. He didn't find any others, but what he did see alarmed him. A number of Mallard ducks had died and had drifted to the edge of the pond at Putah Creek. Usually, carrion eaters quickly claimed any duck meal left unattended, but there were too many dead ducks. Both the dead cats and the dead ducks must have been infected with the same avian flu. In the reports from Asia, cats acquired the virus by eating infected chickens or ducks. He went back to the lab for a plastic sack and surgical gloves and returned to Putah

Creek to pick up the duck carcasses. He would ask Dr. Spitzer to do tissue cultures on them.

Usually migratory birds that carried avian flu were not sick themselves, which allowed them to efficiently spread the virus through their droppings. Apparently, sick migratory birds had weeded themselves out, so that now big flocks were resistant to the virus. Migratory birds congregate in the far north and had quickly spread the disease among themselves, allowing the virus to jump from Asia to Europe or North America via the pole. Flooded rice paddies in the Sacramento River Delta attracted large numbers of migratory birds that probably transmitted the disease to the more domesticated ducks on Putah Creek. A few years before, the Center for Disease Control and Prevention had sent warnings to physicians to be on the lookout for influenza in live poultry handlers, but most physicians and veterinarians were not thinking about avian flu in cats.

The potential of a pandemic worried Dr. Spencer. When he came back, he reviewed what the CDC had reported. The last three worldwide pandemics occurred in 1918, 1957, and 1968, although the last two didn't approach the magnitude of the 1918 disaster when an estimated forty million people died. But the two more recent pandemics were bad enough killing two million and one million respectively. Each time, a new and virulent virus efficiently spreading among humans caused the pandemic, and each time, that new virus was a strain of avian Influenza A.

Avian influenza A viruses do not usually infect humans, but rare cases of human infection have been reported since 1996. Since 2003, health agencies in 14 countries have confirmed 330 cases of human infection with avian Influenza A, subtype H5N1. In most cases, direct contact with sick or dead infected poultry was thought to have been the cause. Estimates of the mortality rate have been as high as 60 percent. Direct human-to-human transmission occurred in only a few cases, although history has shown that genetic mutation, or exchange of genetic material with a human influenza virus, could enhance the efficiency of transmission between humans. Children and young adults suffered the highest mortality rates, because they had never been exposed to any avian influenza virus.

Dr. Spencer knew that the virology lab could not yet confirm the subtype of either Suzie's virus or that of the cats, and since most human Influenza A viruses were not avian flu, he hesitated to act too early. He worried that the press might spread panic over nothing. He needed more time.

Mike Becker came into Dr. Spencer's office.

"Two veterinarians called back and reported several more dead cats, and one of the vets has a sick cat that's still alive. We could get it and do a rapid PCR test."

"A positive test would tell us that the cat had influenza A, but we still can't document cat-to-human transmission until we have the tissue culture results for the subtype. Nevertheless, since cats don't usually get human influenza A, a positive test would strongly suggest avian influenza A. Let's try to get the sick cat."

Mike was back in Dr. Spencer's office in a little more than an hour.

"It's positive! The cat has influenza A pneumonia."

"I'm going to call that pediatrician to see if he's heard anything."

The pediatrician had found out that a colleague was seeing a sick teenager with influenza documented on a PCR test, and she was admitting him to the hospital. The teenager was experiencing respiratory distress from pneumonia. And there was something else: the teenager's family had a cat that they hadn't seen for the past twenty-four hours. The stakes had just risen, and Dr. Spencer told the pediatrician that he was going to call the state.

"We haven't yet documented a match between the virus from the cats and the one in Suzie's specimen, but we have a sick cat with pneumonia and a positive PCR test, and we have electron microscopy evidence of possible influenza infection in two other cats. Cats rarely get influenza, but when they do, Influenza A subtype H5N1 is suspect. Ask your colleague to order a tissue culture on the teenager and have it sent to our lab. We don't know that we have an epidemic yet, but I'm going to call the California State Department of Health and tell them what we know so far. "

They were alarmed. As their first step, they appointed an infection control officer, Dr. Piero Bruni, chairman of the Division of Infectious Disease at the University of California, Davis School of Medicine. His responsibility would be to evaluate the situation and advise both the state and local governments whether, and when, to implement the mitigation guidelines that the Center for Disease Control had issued. He would be in charge of decisions concerning use of the H5N1 vaccine approved by the U.S. Food and Drug Administration and held in stockpile. He would also have to advise about the development of a new vaccine if this outbreak turned out to be subtype H5N1, because the influenza virus in Davis might be a mutant. In addition, Dr. Bruni would decide about the distribution of the drug oseltamivir, the best antimicrobial drug available against influenza viruses. He would also know that resistance to oseltamivir had been reported in some H5N1 cases in Asia.

Mike asked Dr. Spencer what was in the mitigation guidelines. Dr. Spencer had read them when they first came out in 2007 and remembered the key points.

"The CDC refers to their guidelines as a 'social distancing strategy.' What they mean is reduced contact among people, including quarantine. They start with voluntary isolation of cases and all household contacts. Next, they close the schools and cancel public gatherings and offices. They can also limit nonessential movement of people and goods into and out of areas where an outbreak occurs, but I don't know what 'nonessential' means, or who decides."

Mike looked stunned.

"I've got a wife with unstable diabetes and a baby at home in Sacramento."

Dr. Spencer was silent, and then said, "Yes, I know, let's hope this doesn't turn out to be an epidemic."

Late that afternoon, the pediatrician called Dr. Spencer once again.

"Suzie's father, Professor Chandler, called. Suzie is having trouble breathing. I told him I'd meet them at the hospital."

"Thanks for letting me know."

Dr. Bruni called right after.

"Hello, Dr. Spencer, this is Piero Bruni. What can you tell me about these sick cats?"

"We have four cats dead from pneumonia in a period of about forty-eight hours and another cat that looks terminal. The PCR test on the last cat was positive for influenza A. Two children have just been hospitalized for influenza pneumonia, and they both have positive PCR tests for Influenza A, but we don't know if the cats and the children have the same subtype. We started tissue cultures on two of the cats plus one of the children about thirty-six hours ago. This afternoon, we started tissue cultures on the other hospitalized child, a young teenager, and on the carcasses from some ducks at Putah Creek. I'm concerned that we might have a mutant avian virus transmitted from migratory birds to the ducks on Putah Creek, and then to cats that may have eaten sick ducks, and finally to children handling the cats. It sounds like a far-fetched science fiction story, especially because influenza isn't common in cats, but researchers did find avian influenza in cats in China and Southeast Asia a few years ago. I hope the tissue cultures show that the children and the cats have different influenza A viruses, but I'm worried that we may be seeing a very dangerous mutant virus. Have you heard anything about sick or dead birds anywhere else?"

"No, have you?"

"Not yet. If there were anything obvious, I would have expected to hear something from one of the poultry farmers, or perhaps from the rice growers. The rice paddies attract a lot of migratory birds, although most of them are gone by now. I'm worried more about the domestic birds. Wild birds resistant to the virus can transmit it to domestic birds."

"I'm going to have to order that the families of the two sick children be placed in home quarantine for the moment. I'm sure they'll have the children in isolation at the hospital, but I'll verify that just the same. We're going to have to get a warning out to everyone to avoid any contact with cats or birds. That means I'll have to give a full explanation to the press. Meanwhile, you and anyone else who has been in contact with potentially infected animals, or anyone who has been in contact with the two sick children, will have to go into home quarantine. You might as well stay where you are, because everyone in that building ought to be in quarantine."

"I have a veterinary medicine student who has handled the sick cats. He has a wife with unstable diabetes mellitus with frequent insulin reactions, and they have an infant son. They live in an apartment in Sacramento. Do you know anyone who can look after them in case she has an insulin reaction?"

"I'll ask one of our social workers at the hospital in Sacramento to see what she can do. Give me her name and address. Has he been home since handling the infected animals?"

"Yes, he was home last night."

"That complicates matters. Maybe we could set them up in an isolation unit at the UC Davis Medical Center in Sacramento."

"Mike isn't sick. Could we let him go home to his wife and stay with her in quarantine in their apartment in Sacramento?"

"No, I don't want anyone with known contact with this disease to leave Davis. He'll have to stay there."

"I understand. He's going to be very upset, but I'll have to deal with that. I'll let you know when we have the tissue culture results, but it will take a while, you know."

Dr. Spencer called for Mike Becker to come to his office.

"Mike, Dr. Bruni wants everyone who may have been in contact with an infected animal in quarantine. I told him about your wife, and he's going to have one of the social workers at the hospital in Sacramento contact her. Because you've been in contact with them, he's talking about putting them in an isolation unit at the hospital."

"He's taking this pretty seriously, isn't he?"

"I suppose he is."

"Neither of us has any symptoms. Couldn't he just let me go home to look after my wife in the apartment?"

"I've already asked him. He's opposed to anyone leaving Davis who has had known contact with the disease."

"The quarantine is voluntary, isn't it?"

"My recollection is that the CDC guidelines did use the word "voluntary," but I looked up the guidelines on the CDC Web site, and it refers to a document labeled National Strategy for Pandemic Influenza signed by the president. It says, 'Where appropriate, use governmental authorities to limit nonessential movement of people, goods, and services into and out of areas where an outbreak occurs.' The word 'voluntary' is missing. Also, they don't explain what 'nonessential' means, but Dr. Bruni was very clear about what he means."

"This doctor can take away our human rights on the basis of an unproven epidemic?"

"I think the public reaction to this is going to be ugly. The television reporters are going to have a field day with the idea of an avian influenza epidemic in the United States, and people will panic about the risk of spread. If your neighbors in Sacramento discovered that you had been in Davis, and especially that you're associated with the School of Veterinary Medicine, they might very well become aggressive toward you and your wife. I think you'd both be better off if you didn't go home. You can keep in telephone contact with her as often as you like."

"Do you think the virus will spread?"

"In the cases in Asia, the virus never spread beyond a few close contacts between people and infected birds or with sick family members. The two sick children might turn out to be the only cases in Davis. This could all blow over quickly. On the other hand, this virus may have mutated to spread more efficiently than the virus a few years ago in Asia. I don't know what is going to happen."

"I still think this Dr. Bruni is acting rashly."

A few hours later, Dr. Spencer and Mike Baker turned on the six o'clock local news from Sacramento. The station dedicated the entire thirty-minute segment to the "Davis epidemic," showing archive pictures of Putah Creek, the School of Veterinary Medicine, the Davis Community Hospital, and Davis High School where the teenager was a freshman. Dr. Bruni explained the current situation and immediate precautions taken, such as a decision to close all of the schools and nonessential businesses. Then they interviewed the president of the university who announced cancellation of all classes and exams and assured everyone that all university personnel would fully cooperate with the Department of Health. The anchorman explained that the two children in the Davis Community Hospital were in critical condition, and that the little girl's mother, Mrs. Chandler, had become sick as well. Reporters interviewed people on the street in Sacramento who expressed their fears and demanded that the state government quarantine the entire town of Davis.

The national news came on at 6:30 PM, and the "Davis epidemic" was the lead story. Experts from the CDC and the National Institutes of Health explained the risk of avian influenza and described the mitigation guidelines. The reporters interviewing the experts seemed to have little interest in their explanation of the inefficient transmission of the virus among humans in the cases in Asia. Their focus was on the possibility of the virus being a more dangerous mutant.

"If this virus might spread among people as quickly as it spreads among ducks and chickens, does that mean that one person from Davis could infect the whole country?"

"If this epidemic gets a foothold, could the mortality rate become even worse than in 1918?"

"What kind of quarantine restrictions will be in place in Davis?"

By seven o'clock, the police had moved. Farmland completely surrounds the town of Davis, and only a few roads lead out. The California Highway Patrol closed Interstate 80, blocking the freeway at both ends of the town, and then blocked the few secondary roads leading out, too. Vehicles in Davis jammed each blocked road and people began to panic.

"I have to get home to Sacramento. My husband works nights and he needs the car to get to work."

"I was only in Davis for a meeting. If I can't get to work tomorrow, I'll get fired."

"My wife doesn't know I'm in Davis. If she finds out, she'll kill me."

The emergency department at the Davis Community Hospital braced itself for a busy night. Surprisingly, only a few people came. Television viewers knew that people with a dangerous virus were in that hospital. Wikipedia received hundreds of thousands of hits, all on the subject of influenza. Telephone calls to doctors resulted in busy signals. Most people watched television all evening to catch any breaking news. Dr. Spencer spent most of the evening answering calls from reporters and repeating the same story, and Mike Becker dialed his wife frequently and sometimes got through. He and Dr. Spencer served themselves dinner from a vending machine and spent the night on sofas in a lounge at the vet school.

Much had happened on day three, but the news on day four was worse. Early radio and television reports asserted that the teenager admitted to Davis Community Hospital the day before had just died. During the night, the hospital had admitted three more patients, all with pneumonia, all critically ill, and all were freshmen at Davis High School.

At 6:30 AM, Dr. Bruni called Dr. Spencer to ask if anyone had brought in more dead cats or birds.

"No, I'm here with my student, Mike Becker, and it's been very quiet. What have you heard?"

"Several police agencies have picked up a number of people on foot who obviously had come from Davis. From their shoes, it appeared that they had left Davis by avoiding the roads and crossing the fields around the town. They're pretty muddy right now. We've already called the university dorm councillors, who've noted that some students are missing. The university doesn't yet know the number, but apparently it's substantial."

"How about sick people?"

"I've talked briefly with a number of doctors who tell me that large numbers of patients are calling with sore throats, runny noses, or coughs. Some have had mild symptoms for weeks, but a few of them may be acutely ill. All of them want house calls. The physicians will be ordering lots of PCR tests to see if influenza has spread."

"What about oseltamivir?"

"I've arranged for a large supply of the drug to be sent to the Davis Community Hospital. The hospital is small, and so if the number of victims increases rapidly, we'll have to find alternative makeshift hospitals to treat people. We're thinking about using the gymnasiums at the schools and university if the worst happens. Some of the doctors want to treat patients in their homes, but if this epidemic spreads, they may not have the time to be driving all over town."

"Can you get a hold of the stockpiled H5N1 vaccine?"

"It's on the way and should be at the Sacramento International Airport at noon. However, as you know, it may not work because of a possible mutation of the virus, and because the disease might spread too quickly for the vaccine to be effective. We need to work out and publicize a plan to vaccinate everyone in an orderly fashion to avoid a stampede. We may need you to help calm people and explain the plan. I'm holding a conference call at 9:00 AM. It would help if you were on it."

"Yes, of course, I'll be available."

Mike Becker got through on the telephone again to his wife at the UC Davis Medical Center in Sacramento and found that she and their son had spent the night in a small isolation room. She wasn't very happy, but she had not experienced another insulin reaction. Mike tried to explain what was happening, and that so far, only one person had died and just a few others were sick. She wasn't convinced and recounted the news reports about a major epidemic.

Dr. Spencer called his wife who was distraught. She had anguished about little Suzie Chandler, and then early that morning, an ambulance picked up Mrs. Chandler. The paramedics had held an oxygen mask over her face. The two women were good friends, and Mrs. Spencer broke down and cried on the phone. Dr. Spencer felt helpless and just listened to his wife's agonized description of Mrs. Chandler's departure. Nearly everybody in the neighborhood had been in contact with either Suzie or Mrs. Chandler, and now they were all staying indoors.

One of the embittered university employees with crumpled clothes and unshaven stubble had spent a restless night on a cot and approached Dr. Spencer. The employee argued that he didn't have influenza and didn't live in Davis, and didn't see any reason he shouldn't receive a certificate that would allow him to pass through the police line and go to his home in Woodland just ten miles away. Dr. Spencer hadn't slept very well either, but he spent a few minutes with the employee.

"I can't give you that certificate, nor could Dr. Bruni either. Don't you see, none of us has any way to tell if you are infected with the virus or not, because there is a lag time between acquiring the virus and the onset of symptoms. Even if we could give you a certificate, it wouldn't help."

"Why not?"

"Because there are thousands of people in this town who are not infected, and almost all of them would like to leave too."

"Why can't they leave if they don't have influenza?"

"Because none of us can tell who is infected and who isn't. The public health authorities are trying to prevent the disease from spreading all over the country."

"Even if it means sacrificing people who don't yet have influenza?"

"I know that it doesn't seem fair, but we've got to accept the situation as it is."

"That sounds to me like your talking in abstractions. Who gives you or the public health authorities the right to decide who lives and who dies?"

The disgruntled employee left, possibly feeling better, but the conversation had troubled Dr. Spencer. The government was arguing for the greater good for the greater number, but that required denial of the basic right to survival for the individual. Dr. Spencer could not shake himself free from that ethical dilemma. He was tired from his restless night and unable to explain it satisfactorily to himself.

The conference call began promptly at 9:00 AM. On the line were an internist, Dr. James Elliot, who was chairman of the internal medicine division at the Davis Community Hospital, a public health nurse, Mrs. Jane Grace, RN, Dr. John Blackman, president of the university, Mr. Garcia, a public health official placed in charge of obtaining supplies and transportation, and Dr. Spencer. Dr. Bruni gave another update and began assigning tasks.

"Dr. Elliot, you organize the inpatient care and distribution of oseltamivir, which should arrive at the Davis Hospital around noon. Keep me informed about the number of sick patients, their condition, and whether we're going to need to set up a temporary hospital in one of the gymnasiums."

"Mrs. Grace, you recruit as many nurses as you can to set up stations at each school, the civic center, and Rec Hall and Hickey Gym at the university to administer the H5N1 vaccine, which should arrive by late this afternoon. You may want to recruit some teachers, too, to help organize lines and calm the people as they arrive. We're going to receive a large shipment of respirators, which filter out smaller particles better than ordinary facemasks. They will have instructions on how to do 'fit-testing' to assure effective filtering. Perhaps you can teach the teachers how to do it so they can, in turn, teach the people who come in. We also have stacks of pamphlets on hand-washing techniques that they can distribute and explain.

"Mr. Garcia, you need to set up food distribution at the same locations in the schools and keep in touch with Dr. Elliot and Mrs. Grace regarding medical supplies. Be ready to bring in cots and blankets if we have to open temporary hospitals. Trucks will bring in all supplies to the parking lot at Pioneer School just off I-80 at the east end of Davis where you can transfer the supplies to your own trucks for delivery throughout the town.

"Dr. Blackman, people are panicked right now and thinking mostly of saving themselves. Everyone in the community holds you in high esteem, so it would help if you would explain to them the need to help each other in order to survive this crisis. I'd like you to talk to the people on the university radio station this morning and then go to the schools and the hospital to encourage them to pull together.

"Dr. Spencer, I want you to do an assessment of all of the university animal areas for any sign of spread of the virus. And I want you to remain on the line after the conference call."

The call ended except for Dr. Spencer and Dr. Bruni who continued.

"I know we're out on a limb here, but I had to make a decision, because the tissue culture results won't be available until it's too late to have any chance to prevent spread beyond Davis. By the time we find out the subtype of the virus, we'll already know whether the disease is highly contagious or not. One teenager dead and five other very sick victims tell us that this virus is dangerous.

"Everyone now knows that cats may have transmitted this virus to humans. We need to round up all of the stray cats that we can find and destroy them. Also, we have to pick up all animal carcasses of any kind, because if nothing else, dead animals lying around will just contribute to the panic. Can you quietly destroy all of the poultry on the campus farms?"

"Sure, I've already thought of that. We can gas them and then dig a pit with a backhoe to cremate them. I'll try to get some students and employees to help. We have our own respirators, gowns, and gloves. Rounding up stray cats is another story. I don't anticipate much success on that score."

"Is there any way to capture or shoot the ducks around Putah Creek?"

"That's a problem too. If we start shooting, most of them will fly off and become someone else's worry. Of course, we'll pick up any dead ones, and if we can, we'll capture some with nets, but capturing ducks on a pond before they escape will not be any easier than rounding up stray cats."

"OK, do what you can. That brings me to a very unpleasant subject. In the worst case, we might have a large number of people dying in a short period of time. We would have to dispose of the bodies quickly for public health reasons and for psychological reasons. It may never happen, but if it does, we'd better have a plan ready to implement. Your cremation facility at the vet school is the only option for handling a large number of bodies. If you have to, can you handle it?"

Dr. Spencer gulped. "We can do it if we have to."

"Good. The vet school has vans for transporting animals, doesn't it?"

"Yes."

"Can you use them to transport bodies if you have to?"

"Yes."

"If we get into that situation, you'll have to round up helpers with a lot of courage, because they will be putting their lives on the line."

"So will everyone else in Davis."

Dr. Spencer went looking for Mike Becker.

"Dr. Bruni wants us to do a regular survey to look for any sick or dead animals. He is worried about the stray cats throughout the town, but they'll be nearly impossible to trap. We should concentrate first on the poultry and pigs on the university farms. We'll have to cover a lot of territory. Most of the vet students live in university housing or in Davis. Do you think that you could round some up to help?"

"It'll give me something to do. My wife is in good hands, but she's really unhappy, and I can't help worrying."

The rain had started again, so it would be a muddy job. Dr. Spencer switched on the university radio station just as the announcer was finishing reading the plan that Dr. Bruni had e-mailed around the campus. The announcer was explaining about vaccines, respirators, food distribution, and especially about "social distancing." The university president, Dr. Blackman, was about to come on the air.

He gave a quiet, but emotional talk about morality, courage, and service to others, and then called for prayers for the victims who were already suffering from the disease. He warned that many volunteers would be needed if the community were to survive, and explained that the university had set up a Web site that would soon indicate where help was most needed. Many people in the town heard the talk, and most who did considered it the most hopeful few minutes since the epidemic was announced. Others continued with plans for escaping from the town, but even some of those began to waver.

By the middle of the afternoon on the fourth day, nurses at some of the schools had begun injecting the vaccine, and some teachers were already trained to explain to small groups of people how to use the respirators and how to do more effective hand-washing. Food distribution was scheduled to begin the next day. Dr. Elliot called Dr. Bruni to let him know that he had admitted two more influenza victims, both from the same family as one of the high school students admitted earlier. He also reported that Mrs. Chandler had died, and Suzie Chandler was still experiencing some respiratory distress, but not as severe as when she had been admitted to the hospital.

One of the vet students who was helping with the animal survey called Dr. Spencer.

"Mike Becker has a fever. What should we do?"

"Where is he?"

"He's at the avian sciences research facility out by the university airport. He has one of the trucks."

"Can you take me out there? I'll use his truck to take him in to the hospital."

Mike was sick and having trouble breathing. Dr. Spencer used the phone at the avian center to call the hospital to let them know that he was bringing him in. He asked whether the oseltamivir had arrived. It hadn't, but they expected it soon. Mike was shivering and could barely walk to the truck. Dr. Spencer couldn't think of anything to say, except that the antiviral drug was on the way. They were silent for the trip into the hospital.

A nurse took Mike into a wing that was set up to isolate the influenza victims and told Dr. Spencer that he could wait in the main hospital waiting room, and invited him to put on a respirator, gloves, and gown to visit Mike briefly after the doctor saw him.

On the television set in the waiting room, an announcer was talking about the epidemic in a matter-of-fact, detached way, and Dr. Spencer remembered the word "abstraction" that the distraught university employee had used. The voice of the reporter sounded indifferent about the horrible tragedy that was unfolding, as if it were an eclipse of the sun, or a new volcano erupting in a remote area of the Pacific Ocean. Television viewers see terrible tragedies every night with bleak indifference, almost as a sort of entertainment, an electronic Roman coliseum. Dr. Spencer was aware of his own indifference prior to the outbreak, but this tragedy had become personal, and he could no longer steel himself against his own emotional response.

Dr. Blackman, the university president, came into the waiting room having already heard about Mike, the first victim directly associated with the university. Dr Spencer was staring at the floor and had tears in his eyes. He wasn't a religious sort of person, but just then, he needed spiritual comfort, and a university president in a town like Davis is the next best person to a priest in the type of bleak tragedy that was unfolding.

"I've heard that you brought him in, Everett. How is he?"

"He looks awful. He's having trouble breathing. I have to call his wife, who is in isolation at the UC Davis Medical Center in Sacramento. They were together three nights ago, so Dr. Bruni had her placed in isolation because of Mike's contact with sick cats. I'm sure she'll demand to come in, but of course, that will be impossible. On top of everything, Mike and his wife have an infant son to worry about. She's taking insulin for diabetes too."

"How are you, Everett? You did a fine job figuring out the source of the epidemic, and you acted as quickly as you could and probably saved a lot of lives."

"I didn't save Craig Chandler's wife or that poor teenager. Suzie Chandler is still critically ill too. She's in the same unit with Mike."

"You didn't cause that, and you had no way to prevent it. We can control some things in our lives, but not everything. We try to do the best that we can, and you've done your best. You put your life on the line, and because of your example other volunteers in Davis are doing the same. At lot of people are going to survive this epidemic, because enough people care, and enough of them are helping."

"You're very kind. I've got to call Mrs. Becker now."

With some difficulty, he got through to her on the phone. She was alarmed that it was Dr. Spencer who wanted to talk with her.

"Is Mike sick?"

"Yes. I'm with him now at the Davis Community Hospital."

"I knew it! Why couldn't you let him come home?"

"We had great fear that Mike might have brought home the virus to you and your son."

"We didn't catch the virus when he was home three days ago."

"I'm grateful for that."

"I'm coming to Davis!"

"That won't be possible. This virus seems to be highly contagious, and the police won't let anyone leave or enter Davis."

"I want to talk to him."

"The doctors are with him now, and they'll be starting an antiviral drug shortly. As soon as they finish, I'll call you back and give the phone to him."

Distress took many forms during this epidemic, but the deepest, as well as the most widespread, was separation. The telephones helped, but everyone still assumed the worse, because the invisible killer had no respect for morality or justice. The virus was indifferent, just like television viewers watching the epidemic from afar. People coming into the centers for the vaccine, respirators, and food could see each other, and they knew that most were still healthy. Outside of Davis, relatives and friends saw only the television images that painted a desperate picture, and they heard the announcers who emphasized words like contagion, epidemic, and mortality.

A nurse came out to invite Dr. Spencer in to see Mike, who continued to experience respiratory distress and wore an oxygen mask. An X-ray technician had just taken a portable chest X-ray to avoid moving Mike out of the quarantine area of the hospital and into the radiology unit to reduce the risk of contagion to other hospitalized patients. The oseltamivir had finally arrived, and the pharmacy was sending it up.

Dr. Spencer asked the nurse if it would be possible for Mike to talk to his wife on the phone. Mike heard and began nodding his head vigorously, then took off his oxygen mask and said, "Please let me talk to her!" The nurse looked anxious, but realized that it might be now or never. They put the call through, and Dr. Spencer and the nurse moved away from the bed a little.

Dr. Elliot came in and spoke quietly with the nurse and Dr. Spencer.

"He's in quite a bit of respiratory distress and the portable chest X-ray shows bilateral bronchopneumonia. His arterial oxygen level is holding up, but that usually doesn't start to drop until late. The PCR test for influenza A was positive, of course. We'll be giving him the oseltamivir in just a minute. I hope it works, because he's very sick."

Mike was talking on the phone and crying and gasping. Dr. Spencer and the nurse had to look away. They both had tears in their eyes. Dr. Elliot asked Mike gently to end the call so that he could replace the oxygen mask, and then asked Dr. Spencer to allow Mike to rest.

Dr. Spencer called back to the veterinary school, and one of the vet students answered the phone on the first ring instead of one of the secretaries.

"How's Mike?"

"He's very sick, but they have him on oxygen, and he has an IV running. They've just started the oseltamivir."

"It sounds bad."

"We may not know for a while. How's the cat roundup and poultry extermination going?"

"A lot of people have volunteered. We found many more duck carcasses at Putah Creek, but when we approached the pond, the rest took off. We've cleaned up all of the dead ones and then decided to leave the area so that the ducks would come back. We think that's better than to let them spread the virus somewhere else. On the other hand, we're batting zero capturing stray cats. Maybe we can trap some using food as bait, but I don't think we'll be able to catch very many."

"We didn't find any sick birds anywhere on the university farms, but we're setting up now to gas the poultry buildings, and a backhoe is digging a pit. It will be dark soon, so we might not be able to finish until tomorrow morning. I hate to destroy so many healthy birds, but I understand the risk of not doing it."

"Everybody understands how to protect himself?"

"Nobody is taking any unnecessary risks. People want to help, but they also want to live."

Dr. Spencer worried. Contagious diseases can find their mark sooner or later no matter how stringent the precautions. Yet, if the community were to survive, the work had to be done. What was truly remarkable was that so many volunteers had stepped up; there was no lack of people to do these unpleasant and high-risk duties. The student volunteers were spending only a few years in Davis. Still they were risking their lives to help people they didn't even know. Mike Becker's illness had made this a personal crusade for the volunteers.

The night passed quietly, and Dr. Elliot admitted no more influenza victims to the hospital. Dr. Bruni estimated that the nurses had administered vaccines to nearly half of the community by working through the evening. Some nurses worked through the night as long as people kept coming. A full complement of nurses would be ready to immunize the rest of the community the next morning.

On the morning of the fifth day, the devastating news came from the hospital that Mike Becker and one of the high school students had died. Miraculously, Suzie Chandler was improving, and the other patients were stable for the moment, but of the nine people who required hospitalization, four were now dead.

The campus remained very quiet as most people were staying home. Some came to the schools and gymnasiums to pick up food, but they were all wearing respirators and keeping their distance. A few noticed the black smoke that trailed into the sky from the west end of town near the animal research areas. Dr. Blackman came on the radio again to praise the volunteers and to emphasize the lack of new cases of influenza overnight.

The work of rounding up cats and ducks continued, but with little success. Dr. Spencer spent most of the day at home with his wife, since little remained for him to do, and both were supposed to be in quarantine. Mostly they read—or rather they tried to read, but did not comprehend the words. Mrs. Spencer cried a little.

Doctors found that they did have time for house calls after all, but only a few patients called. Oddly, no one complained of an acute onset of a fever, sore throat, or cough. Perhaps "social distancing" had suppressed transmission of other viral illnesses, or maybe people feared that a doctor pronouncing a sentence of influenza would net them a trip to an isolation ward at the hospital. Since no further patients required admission to the hospital, Dr. Elliot had plenty of time to care for the five remaining victims and to reassure their families. Mrs. Grace, the public health nurse, continued her task of making Davis a model hand-washing community, and Dr. Bruni held his breath.

Several more quiet days passed, and people began to gather to talk, although at a respectable distance. No one needed reminding about the policy of "social distancing," and everyone continued to wear a respirator, at least outside in public. Neighbors forged new bonds as survivors who had experienced the Davis epidemic. People had forgotten Christmas lights, but now they began to reappear. Then the mayor ordered turning back on the holiday lights in the commercial center of the town even though all of the stores remained closed.

In the dorms and in apartment buildings surrounding the campus, the barrage of disturbing news had fatigued the students, who began venturing away from their television sets. Some took walks on the campus even though they still had final exams remaining for the quarter, but the university had postponed all exams until after the outbreak ended, whenever that would be.

The television channels still covered the epidemic on all of the newscasts, but other stories displaced it as the lead story. Good news is bad news in the reporting business. As it became more evident that the worst had passed, the governor of California came on television to praise the volunteers as heroes who had saved their community and prevented the spread to the rest of the state, and possibly even to the rest of the world. Drs. Bruni, Spencer, and Elliot were not as certain as the governor about why the outbreak had suddenly ceased. Perhaps their efforts had worked, but they just didn't know.

By Christmas, there were still no new cases, and Dr. Bruni lifted the quarantine. Davis remained very quiet during Christmas week, but then at least half of the population usually leaves at that time for wherever they call home. A memorial service was planned for the victims, but postponed until after New Year's Day to allow everyone to attend. Dr. Bruni had quietly suggested the postponement to avoid any large gathering of people.

The day after Christmas, Dr. Spitzer reported the findings of the viral tissue cultures on duck carcasses, cats, and human victims. All were positive for Influenza A, subtype H5N1, the same subtype that had killed most of the victims of avian influenza in Asia during the prior decade. Two poultry farms in California, one near Merced and the other near Visalia, noted a die-off of chickens. Government workers destroyed all of the poultry on those farms and on the ones surrounding. They sent specimens to the viral lab at UC Davis, and in the middle of January, the results came back Influenza A, subtype H5N1. There were no human cases.

The Center for Disease Control listed the Davis epidemic as the seventh outbreak of subtype H5N1 around the world, and the first in the Western Hemisphere. Why did the epidemic in Davis erupt so suddenly, and then die out just as quickly as had happened in Asia? Some scientists postulated that the virus was not as efficient in jumping to other species as feared. Others said that the number of ducks on Putah Creek was not large enough to spread the disease. Still others thought that too many links limited the outbreak. First the virus had to spread among wild birds, then jump to the domesticated ducks on Putah Creek, infect the feral cats that ate the ducks, and finally pass to humans who handled the cats. Infectious disease experts were just as puzzled, and just as relieved, as those who had analyzed the outbreaks of avian flu in Asia a few years before.

Several of the victims had never handled any infected animals, but had been in contact with other human victims documented to have had the virus. So what prevented further spread between humans? The citizens in Davis convinced themselves that the preventive precautions taken and the large numbers of volunteers had blocked the spread and prevented a major epidemic.

For the winter quarter, enrollment at UC Davis dropped, as many students found other universities to continue their studies. All of the students at the School of Veterinary Medicine returned. In fact, many of them never left during the holidays even after Dr. Bruni had lifted the quarantine. Never was there a group of vet students with stronger ties.

Fewer visitors attended Picnic Day that year, but the parade was bigger and better than ever before. Every civic and university service group had gained members and was marching. The crowd cheered the car with Dr. Blackman at the front of the parade, and later, a group of nurses and teachers who had volunteered at the schools and gymnasiums received a rousing ovation. But the most emotional response came for a modest float that the School of Veterinary Medicine sponsored—no cheering, just quiet applause and tears.

Davis was recovering.

About the Author

Blair Beebe, MD, was born in Camden, New Jersey, in 1938, and graduated from Penn State University prior to entering Jefferson Medical College in Philadelphia in 1959. As a medical student, he served an externship working in the emergency room of Underwood Hospital, a "cottage hospital" in Woodbury, New Jersey. After graduation from Jefferson in 1963, he completed an internship in Philadelphia and then attended the U.S. Navy School of Aviation Medicine in Pensacola, Florida, and served for two years as a flight surgeon during the Vietnam War in carrier squadron VAP-61. At the end of his tour of duty in Southeast Asia in 1967, he completed three more years of residency training in internal medicine in California, and then entered practice with the Keene Clinic in Keene, New Hampshire. He served as chairman of the Medical Division during the closure of the old Elliot Community Hospital and transition to the new Dartmouth-affiliated Cheshire Hospital in Keene.

In 1973 he returned to California where he served as assistant physician-in-chief at the Kaiser Permanente Medical Center, Santa Clara, and at the same time, held a teaching post in the Division of Endocrinology and Metabolism at Stanford University. In 1980 he became physician-in-chief of the new Kaiser Permanente Medical Center in San Jose, and in 1990 was named associate executive director of the Permanente Medical Group in the Northern California Region.

Dr. Beebe is certified by the American Board of Internal Medicine and a fellow of the American College of Physicians. He also holds a Master of Liberal Arts degree from Stanford University. During the 1990s he served on the Medical Advisory Committee of the Technology Evaluation Center at the Blue Cross/Blue Shield Association in Chicago, and was senior clinical consultant to Computer Sciences Corporation, San Francisco. He is the author of several medical journal articles and the recent book, *The Hundred-Year Diet* (2008). Dr. Beebe lives in Portola Valley, California, with his wife Sue, and has four children, one of whom is a pediatrician in the Permanente Medical Group. Three of their children are graduates of the University of California at Davis, and one currently teaches English at Davis High School. Two sons are experts in computer graphics and computer animation at Silicon Valley companies.

CPSIA information can be obtained at www.ICGtesting.com
Printed in the USA
LVOW040822020312

271221LV00001B/58/P